POCKET ROUGH GUIDE
HONG KONG
& MACAU

written and researched by
DAVID LEFFMAN

CONTENTS

HONG KONG AND MACAU

Facing each other across the Pearl River estuary, Hong Kong and Macau offer an exciting yet easy entry into the Chinese world. Colonies of Britain and Portugal respectively until they were returned to mainland China in the 1990s as Special Administrative Regions (SARs), today their southern Chinese heritage is increasingly apparent. Among the hi-tech infrastructure and the population's Westernized outlook, conservative traditions persist, from shrines to the god of wealth and age-old festivals, to the way contemporary architectural design takes principles such as *feng shui* into account. Former colonial ties are most obvious in the fact that many people speak English as well as Cantonese, and in Macau's decidedly un-Chinese antique buildings.

Lok Ke Wan beach

Tai Mo Shan

Hong Kong's famously futuristic harbourside architecture has long set the standard for similar cityscapes rearing up all over Asia. There's also a broad mix of other architectural styles here, encompassing Mong Kok's ramshackle town housing, traditional clan villages in the New Territories, Tai O's stilt-houses and the centuries-old temples which are dotted around. The accompanying markets and street life are compellingly frenetic, while the shopping – though no longer a bargain – offers the chance to compare a vast range of products sold everywhere from open-air stalls to hi-tech malls. Hong Kong is also one of the best places in the world to eat Cantonese food, while the territory's Western influence means there's a plentiful selection of bars and nightspots.

Surprisingly, Hong Kong's outlying areas remain fairly undeveloped, with a countryside of beaches, rugged hills, wild coastline and islands – although none of it especially remote – where you can escape the pace and claustrophobia of the downtown areas. Hong Kong's only real downside is that the overwhelming commercialism and consumption make it hard to engage with the underlying

When to visit

Hong Kong and Macau are **tropical**, which means generally humid conditions throughout the year. From December to February is the coolest period (16ºC), though usually dry; temperatures rise from March through to May (23ºC) and rainfall increases; while from June until September the weather is steaming hot (30ºC), often with fearsome **typhoons** (from the Chinese *tai fung* – "big wind"), whose storms affect sea traffic. Tourist levels are even year-round, but book accommodation in advance, especially for international sporting events and for Chinese New Year in January or February.

What's new

Limited space and a craze for cutting-edge architecture means that large-scale land reclamation and enormous construction projects have long been a fact of life in Hong Kong. Current builds include a third airport runway, an Imperial Palace Museum at West Kowloon (see page 71) and, most ambitiously, a 55km-long road bridge west across the Pearl River estuary to the Chinese city of Zhuhai (see page 112).

Chinese culture – though you can glimpse it at Happy Valley's horse races, Mong Kok's Bird Market or simply by watching early-morning tai chi practitioners going through their routines in Kowloon Park. Cultural barriers also drop at the several annual Chinese festivals sprinkling the calendar – Chinese New Year, the Dragon Boat Races and Cheung Chau Bun Festival are the liveliest – when even visitors will find it hard not to get caught up in the action.

Smaller and more visually attractive than its neighbour, Macau is also ethnically Chinese, but its charms rest more on its backdrop of old Portuguese churches, forts and streets, which lend the place a colonial-tropical ambiance. Its tiny scale means you can see just about everything on an easy day-trip from Hong Kong, while its superb food marries Portuguese, Chinese, Goan, Brazilian and African influences, washed down with Portuguese port and brandy. As far as the Chinese are concerned, however, Macau's main appeal is in its many casinos – it's the only place on Chinese territory where they are legal – which draw in swarms of punters from Hong Kong and mainland China.

Grand Lisboa Casino, Macau

Where to...

Shop

Thanks to internet shopping, the affordable electronics gear Hong Kong was once famous for is no longer a particularly good deal, though you will be able to lay your hands on just about every model and brand of computer, camera, smartphone and tablet available at specialist warehouses in Wan Chai, Mong Kok and Sham Shui Po. Jewellery shops are everywhere in Central, Tsim Sha Tsui and Mong Kok, and the same goes for clothing, with various bargains available in Mong Kok, Sham Shui Po and on Ap Lei Chau island. If you're looking to shop for art or antiques, head to the dozens of galleries strung along Hollywood Road.

OUR FAVOURITES: Lok Man Rare Books, see page 41. Elissa Cohen Jewellery, see page 72. Yue Po Chai Antiques, see page 43.

Drink

Macau has no real drinking culture, but Hong Kong's bar scene focuses on Lan Kwai Fong in Central, where dozens of lively bars and pubs compete for the swarms of yuppies, office workers, expats and tourists that descend nightly. It's not hard to find somewhere to fit your mood, be it sports bar, Irish pub or quiet terrace. Serious drinkers – mostly expats – gravitate east to seedier Wan Chai, while across the harbour in Tsim Sha Tsui you'll find a thin scattering of Brit-style pubs. Bars open from late afternoon through to the early hours; drinks are pricey, so look out for happy hours.

OUR FAVOURITES: Club 71, see page 46. Delaney's, see page 75. Felix, see page 74.

Eat

In Hong Kong, the downtown areas – Hong Kong Island's north shore between Sheung Wan and Causeway Bay, and the Kowloon peninsula opposite, including Tsim Sha Tsui, Jordan and Mong Kok – are absolutely jammed with restaurants. These cover all budgets and, along with native Cantonese cooking, a range of international cuisines. In Macau the bias is towards Portuguese and indigenous Macanese dishes, with restaurants thickest around Largo do Senado, though don't overlook village locations at Taipa and Coloane. Wherever you eat, expect brusque service, little elbow room and a hot and noisy atmosphere, just how the Chinese like it.

OUR FAVOURITES: Bowrington Road Market, see page 55. Yan Toh Heen, see page 75. Clube Militar, see page 122.

Go out

Clubs in Hong Kong fire up after about 9pm, though as most are located in the city's bars, you can often get drinks before the music kicks off. Expect DJs or house bands playing mainstream rock through to punk and jazz; Lan Kwai Fong's bars lend themselves to more intimate events, with larger clubs and dance floors in Wan Chai and Tsim Sha Tsui's Knutsford Terrace. Hong Kong doesn't see many big international acts, though Cantopop and Mandopop stars – from Hong Kong, China and Taiwan – play at the Hong Kong Coliseum or Queen Elizabeth Stadium.

OUR FAVOURITES: Magnum Club see page 47. Vibes, see page 75. Fringe Club, see page 46.

Hong Kong and Macau at a glance

Shenzhen Bay

Yuen Long

Kam Tin

The New Territories p.86.
Escape downtown Hong Kong's crowds and urban claustrophobia in this mix of open spaces, wild coastline, antique fortified villages and countryside hikes.

Tuen Mun

◁ Macau p.108.
Don't miss Macau's eighteenth-century churches and massive stone forts, its buzzing casino district and unique blend of colonial Portuguese and Chinese food.

Ma Wan

Chek Lap Kok

✈ Hong Kong International Airport

Hong Kong Disneyland

Discovery Bay

Tung Chung

Peng Chau

Lantau

Silvermine Bay

▲ *Tai Tung Shan*

Mui Wo

Hei Ling Chau

▲ *Lantau Peak*

Cheung Chau

Lantau p.98.
Hong Kong's largest island is crowned by its largest Buddha statue, reached via a half-hour cable-car ride offering staggering views.

Lamma and Cheung Chau p.104.
Small, quiet islands home to local fishing communities, offering fine seafood, colourful history, easy walks and the Tai Chiu Bun Festival.

Kowloon: Jordan to Diamond Hill p.76.
Traditional street markets specializing in clothes, jade and even goldfish, with some underplayed cultural gems hidden away on the outskirts.

Hong Kong Island: Central to Kennedy Town p.26.
Hong Kong Island's crowded, upmarket business and shopping district, featuring futuristic skyscrapers, a lively bar scene and stunning cityscapes from The Peak.

Kowloon: Tsim Sha Tsui p.64.
More staggering views and an unbelievable density of tourist shopping opportunities, plus a clutch of excellent museums for wet weather.

Hong Kong Island: Wan Chai, Causeway Bay and Happy Valley p.48.
A bland strip of wide arterial roads and department stores, sporting ever more bars and shopping opportunities – plus the raucously entertaining Happy Valley Racetrack.

▲ Tai Mo Shan

Shing Mun Reservoir

Tsuen Wan

Amah Rock ▲

Lion Rock ▲

Sham Shui Po

Tsim Sha Tsui

Sheung Wan

Central District

Kennedy Town

The Peak

Wan Chai

Causeway Bay

Shau Kei Wan

Hong Kong Island

Aberdeen

Deep Water Bay

Ocean Park

Ap Lei Chau

Yung Shue Wan

Repulse Bay

Repulse Bay

Stanley

Shek O

N

Lamma

Sok Kwu Wan

0	kilometres	4
0	miles	2

Hong Kong Island: The South Side p.58.
Floating restaurants, a wonderful theme park for the kids, some hiking and unexpectedly good beaches – Hong Kong Island's south coast has it all.

15

Things not to miss

It's not possible to see everything that Hong Kong and Macau has to offer in one trip – and we don't suggest you try. What follows is a selective taste of the region's highlights, from its dazzling architecture to markets galore.

> **Views from The Peak**
See page 36
Almost all of Hong Kong is visible from Victoria Peak, with a staggering view north across the harbour, Kowloon and into the New Territories.

< **Star Ferry**
See page 26
This evocative ride across Victoria Harbour allows water-level views of shipping activity, framed by row upon row of Central's hi-tech towers.

∨ **São Paulo façade**
See page 109
Macau's most famous colonial Portuguese building, though only the intricately carved stonework shell remains after a fire in 1835.

< Maritime Museum
See page 26
Hong Kong's exciting seafaring
history – including its involvement
in everything from the opium
trade to piracy and warfare – is
thoroughly explored at this excellent
museum, using contemporary
maps, photographs and models.

∨ Lan Kwai Fong
See page 33
Unwind over a drink or two at the
heart of Hong Kong's club and bar
scene – a score of riotous dens
provide booze and music until the
small hours.

< Fireworks at Chinese New Year

See page 142

Hong Kong and Macau usher in the Chinese New Year with brilliantly intense firework displays – Hong Kong's in particular is like spending forty minutes in the middle of a war zone.

∨Yum cha

See page 44

Sample this classic Cantonese meal (also known as *dim sum*) at a teahouse, where a host of small sweet and savoury dumplings are accompanied by a pot of fragrant tea. A good bet is the *Lin Heung Tea House*.

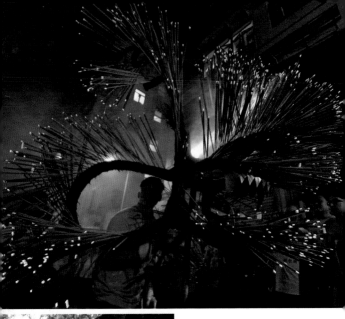

∧ Tai Hang Fire Dragon
See page 143
Forty metres of smoking, glowing dragon, studded with incense sticks, is paraded through this Hong Kong Island suburb after dark during the Mid-Autumn Festival. Come prepared for the crowds.

< Picnic at Bride's Pool
See page 94
Pleasant, popular woodland picnic area with waterfalls and streams, easily reached by bus from Tai Po market via the hamlet of Tai Mei Tuk.

∧ **Ocean Park**
See page 59
Hong Kong's first theme park, complete with pandas, Chinese alligators and a huge array of fun (and soaking wet) rides.

∨ **Roasted meats**
See page 45
Cantonese cooking excels in roasted goose, pigeon and pork, the latter served thinly sliced or incorporated into buns or pastries. Best experienced at a *yum cha* session or at specialist restaurants like *Yung Kee*.

∧ Temple Street Night Market
See page 76
Fun, touristy night market, good for a souvenir, an alfresco meal or even an impromptu performance of Cantonese opera.

< Macanese food
See page 123
Restaurants such as *Litoral* provide mammoth portions of Macau's unique dishes, including "African Chicken" and feijoada (bean and sausage stew).

< **Sham Shui Po**
See page 81
Ramshackle run of budget
haberdashery and discounted
clothing stores, with an interesting
flea market in nearby Ap Liu
Street.

∨ **Three Lamps District**
See page 114
Macau's answer to Hong Kong's
Sham Shui Po – copious fruit and
veg, plus clothing stalls with cut-
price rates and an eccentric range
of sizes and fittings.

THINGS NOT TO MISS

Day One in Hong Kong

Victoria Park. See page 50. Begin the day watching tai chi practitioners performing their slow-motion shadow-boxing routines in downtown Hong Kong's largest public space.

Times Square. See page 51. This is what Hong Kong is all about: cruising fashion boutiques in huge, multilevel malls.

Queen's Road East. See page 48. A kilometre of quirky shops and the unusual Pak Tai and Hung Shing temples – not to mention Tai Yuen Street's lively outdoor market.

Hong Kong Park. See page 34. Attractive landscaped hillside right above busy Queensway; spot colourful tropical birds inside the walk-through Edward Youde Aviary. Begin the day watching tai chi practitioners performing their slow-motion shadow-boxing routines in downtown Hong Kong's largest public space.

Victoria Park

Lunch. See page 44. Drop into the *Lok Cha Tea House* at the K.C. Lo Gallery, for vegetarian *dim sum*.

Bank of China tower. See page 32. This knife-shaped tower is a major player in the *feng shui* wars being waged in Hong Kong's competitive financial district.

Hollywood Road. See page 36. Antique stores, curio shops and art galleries surround the smoky Man Mo Temple, dedicated to the twin gods of war and culture.

Queen's Road East

Sheung Wan Market. See page 38. A wholesale market for dried medicinal herbs, seafood and animal products.

Dinner. See page 45. Time for a Cantonese blowout on roast goose at *Yung Kee* restaurant in Central, before hitting Lan Kwai Fong for a nightcap.

Hollywood Road

Day Two in Hong Kong

Kam Tin. See page 87. Start your day with a visit to this old walled clan village, famous for resisting the British takeover of the New Territories in 1897 – at which point the iron gates were confiscated.

Wishing Trees. See page 93. Hong Kong's folk beliefs are on display at these two fig trees, known as the Wishing Trees, where people write wishes on strips of red paper and attach them to notice boards.

Hong Kong Wetland Park. See page 88. With bird hides, a butterfly garden and an excellent aquarium, Hong Kong Wetland Park provides a fun insight into the Chinese take on the natural world.

Wishing Trees

Lunch There aren't many restaurants in this part of the New Territories, so pack a picnic and make use of the outdoor tables in Hong Kong Wetland Park.

Mong Kok markets. See page 77. After lunch, head back to town and mix with the crowds searching for bargains, or a pet, at Mong Kok's Goldfish and Ladies' markets.

Temple Street Night Market. See page 76. Souvenirs, alfresco dining, fortune-telling and Cantonese opera – this fun, hectic and noisy market is more like street theatre, and it's not one you'll want to miss.

Hong Kong Wetland Park

Dinner. See page 76. Hong Kong offers great seafood, so knuckle down with the locals at Temple Street Night Market's outdoor tables, and feast on chilli crab, steamed shellfish and fresh grilled snapper.

Kowloon Walled City Park. See page 81. Go for a post-dinner wander around this shanty-town-turned-city-park and wind down the day by taking a look at the photo collection of the Walled City.

Temple Street Night Market

Natural Hong Kong

Nature might seem far away in Hong Kong, but there are still a few places to enjoy the great outdoors – and perhaps even spot some wildlife.

Kadoorie Farm. See page 94. Easily reached by bus from Tai Po, this working organic farm is home to dozens of injured and orphaned animals, including birds of prey, wild boar and reclusive, tiny muntjac deer.

Pink-dolphin spotting. See page 102. Take a boat out to look for these rare creatures – adults truly are a lurid pink – of which only about sixty survive in the waters around Hong Kong, mostly seen off western Lantau.

Tai Long Wan beach. See page 96. Probably the longest, most secluded strip of sand in all Hong Kong, Tai Long Wan beach is popular with surfers, though take note that getting here from Sai Kung town requires a little pre-planning.

Hong Kong Wetland Park. See page 88. Accessible fringe of a saltwater estuary up along the Chinese border, dotted with shallow ponds and hides, where you can spot a host of winter migrants – including, with luck, rare black-faced spoonbills.

Lunch. See page 94. Pack a lunch and head to Bride's Pool. This pleasant, popular woodland picnic area also features waterfalls and streams, and is easily reached by bus from Tai Po market via the hamlet of Tai Mei Tuk.

Dragon's Back hike. See page 61. An easy introduction to Hong Kong's hiking potential, this two-hour trail leads over a wild headland and down to an attractive beach. If you time things right, then you can enjoy a meal at a local restaurant afterwards.

Pink-dolphin spotting

Tai Long Wan beach

Dragon's Back hike

Island life

Lamma, Cheung Chau and Lantau – by far the largest of Hong Kong's mostly uninhabited islands – are all connected by regular ferry services from the downtown areas.

Lamma and Cheung Chau. See page 104. Kick off at either of these small islands, once home to piratical fishing communities, but now better known for their beaches, quiet back lanes and waterfront restaurants dishing up excellent seafood. In April/May, Cheung Chau host their bizarre Tai Chiu Bun Festival (see below).

Tian Tan Big Buddha, Lantau. See page 100. Seated serenely above the Po Lin Monastery, this immense bronze sculpture is one of Hong Kong's iconic landmarks. Don't forget to enjoy a vegetarian lunch at the monastery afterwards.

Tian Tan Big Buddha

Tai O, Lantau. See page 101. One of Hong Kong's last old-style fishing villages, famed for its fermented prawn paste, sour fruit drinks and dried fish, where many of the houses are built on stilts over the water.

Lantau Peak, Lantau. See page 99. Make the steep but relatively easy climb up 934m-high Lantau Peak, the second highest summit in Hong Kong – it's best just before dawn, so you can watch the sunrise.

Tai O

Ngong Ping 360 Cablecar, Lantau. See page 98. Enjoy unparalleled views of Lantau's mountains – and the airport – from this 5.7km-long cablecar ride between the MTR station at Tung Chung and the Po Lin Monastery.

Tai Chiu Bun Festival, Cheung Chau. See page 107. In April/May, thousands head to Cheung Chau's Tai Chiu Bun Festival; featuring martial arts displays, a street parade of brightly-dressed children, and a bizarre midnight race to climb a gigantic tower of steamed buns.

Ngong Ping 360 Cablecar

Old Macau

Old Macau's Portuguese-influenced cathedrals, forts and cobbled lanes make a complete break from the hi-tech, modern towers dominating Hong Kong's harbour.

Largo do Senado. See page 108. Begin your day by heading to Old Macau's main square, sided in pastel-coloured religious institutions and arcaded shops.

São Paulo façade. See page 109. Landmark frontage of a seventeenth-century cathedral, all that remains after a devastating fire in 1835.

Fortaleza do Monte. See page 110. There are great views from this seventeenth-century fort, which is complete with old cannons and a museum outlining Macau's lively history.

Largo do Senado

Leal Senado. See page 108. Browse the art gallery and decorative Portuguese tiling inside Macau's one-time seat of government.

 Lunch. See page 122. Lunch on coffee and *nata*, Portuguese custard tarts, at *Café Ou Mun*.

Rua da Felicidade. See page 116. Macau's former red-light district is now a busy street of hotels, restaurants and *pastelarias* selling almond biscuits and roasted meats.

Rua da Felicidade

Largo do Lilau. See page 117. Picturesque residential square in the Barra, one of the first to be settled by Europeans and includes a spring seeping out of a wall-fountain.

A-Ma Temple. See page 117. The A-Ma Temple is the site of the oldest temple in Macau, dedicated to the southern Chinese protector of sailors and fishermen.

 **Dinner**. See page 123. Dig into some of the city's finest indigenous Macanese cooking at *Litoral*, near the old harbour.

Restaurant Litoral

Budget Hong Kong

Hong Kong is generally considered an expensive place to visit, but there are plenty of free (or nearly free) sights and activities, if you know where to look.

Zoological and Botanical Gardens. See page 34. Shaded city park with decorative flowers, orangutans, gibbons, lemurs and cages of birds.

Edward Youde Aviary. See page 35. Huge walk-through aviary with balconies at canopy height, allowing close-up encounters with birdlife.

Views from The Peak. See page 36. Pay a few dollars for the bus – or walk up for a challenge – and The Peak offers superlative vistas over this dynamic city.

Lunch. See page 45. *Tsui Wah* is a budget Hong Kong institution: three floors of trademark fishball soups, Hainan chicken rice and fried noodles.

Viewing Bay, Central Plaza. See page 48. Head to Wan Chai's Central Plaza, Floor 46, during office hours for superb free views of the harbour and Peak.

Star Ferry. See page 26. Pay a pittance to enjoy one of the world's most iconic views: Victoria Harbour from the water.

Kowloon Park martial arts performances. See page 70. Martial artists demonstrate their prowess every Sunday afternoon; the shows finish with colourful lion dances.

Mong Kok Goldfish Market. See page 77. Probably the most offbeat of Hong Kong's traditional street markets, where these lucky fish are traded in quantity.

Dinner. See page 85. Queue up to eat at the world's cheapest Michelin-star rated restaurant, *Tim Ho Wan*.

Edward Youde Aviary

Martial arts performance, Kowloon Park

Dim sum, Tim Ho Wan

PLACES

Tai Mo Shan sunset

Hong Kong Island: Central to Kennedy Town

Set on Hong Kong Island's north shore, Central and the adjoining districts are where the city coalesced after Hong Kong was seized by the British in 1841. Businesses blossomed between Victoria Harbour and The Peak's steep lower slopes, a narrow strip with so little room that buildings had no choice but to evolve upwards into a forest of tall concrete and glass towers interconnected by a web of elevated walkways. Central's atmosphere is contemporary and upmarket: banks all have their headquarters here, shopping opportunities are high-end, and it throngs with clubs, bars and restaurants. For a contrast, seek out older buildings or unwind in Hong Kong Park, while a trip up The Peak offers superlative views of the city and a real break from the crush at street level.

The Star Ferry

MAP P.28, POCKET MAP A18
Central/Tsim Sha Tsui. ⓦ starferry.com.hk/
en/home. Daily 6.30am–11.30pm, every
6–12min. Lower deck $2.20, upper deck
$2.70.

By far the best way to arrive in Central is by **Star Ferry** over from

The Star Ferry

Tsim Sha Tsui, dodging container ships and coastal vessels along the way. The sight of Central's skyscrapers, framed by the hills and looming up as the ferry makes its seven-minute crossing of busy Victoria Harbour, is one of the most thrilling images of Hong Kong, especially when the buildings are lit up after dark. The portly vessels, each named *Evening Star, Northern Star* etc, have been running since 1898, and the current 1950s-style green-and-cream livery together with wooden decks and seating are charmingly anachronistic. This isn't just a tourist sight though – the double-decker boats carry about one hundred thousand passengers a day, mostly locals, so come prepared for crowds.

Maritime Museum

MAP P.28, POCKET MAP F5
Central Pier 8, next to the Star Ferry pier
ⓣ 3713 2500 ⓦ hkmaritimemuseum.
org. Mon–Fri 9.30am–5.30pm, Sat & Sun
10am–7pm. $30; free on Wed.

Victoria Harbour

Central is the best place to ponder Hong Kong's magnificent **Victoria Harbour**, from whose Cantonese label (*Heung Gang* or Fragrant Harbour) the entire SAR takes its name. This safe haven for shipping was what drew the British to the island in the first place, and after the colony became established, international trading concerns – which at the time depended entirely on maritime transport – were naturally attracted here. Today, Hong Kong's money-making enterprises have shifted into Central's towers, and the harbour is shrinking as land is reclaimed in order to build still more skyscrapers: at 1km across, the harbour is half as wide as in 1840. This narrowing has reduced the harbour's ability to flush itself clean, though since 2015 sewage – once pumped raw into the water – has been treated first at a plant on nearby Stonecutters Island. Despite this, it's still difficult to beat the thrill of crossing the harbour by boat; alternatively, you can walk along Central's landscaped waterfront or Tsim Sha Tsui's Avenue of Stars for a view of the maritime activity that originally made Hong Kong great – junks, ferries, motorboats, container ships, cruise liners and sailing boats all pass through. This is one of the busiest ports in the world, used by around five hundred thousand vessels every year.

Hong Kong's long heritage of maritime trade, piracy and war is given a thorough airing at the well-planned **Maritime Museum**, and it's not difficult to spend an hour or more here. High points include the scores of **models** – some unearthed from 2000-year-old tombs, others lovingly crafted from wood – covering every known type of Chinese craft; beautifully illuminated **antique maps** of the nearby coast and cities; paintings of eighteenth-century Chinese ports by Gentiloni; export porcelain salvaged from local shipwrecks; and a nineteenth-century bronze cannon used during the **Opium Wars** (during which Hong Kong was taken as a prize by the British). The upstairs displays are less relevant, but the feature windows here allow fantastic, unobstructed views across harbour.

Harbourfront Promenade

MAP P.28, POCKET MAP D4–F5

This landfill project, over ten years in the making and still awaiting final landscaping, comprises a kilometre or so of waterfront area between Central's piers and Wanchai's Convention Centre. The only landmark as such is the 60m-tall **Observation Wheel**, though this has been closed indefinitely by a long-running dispute over ownership.

IFC2 and Exchange Square

MAP P.28, POCKET MAP E5
Connaught Rd and Finance St Ⓜ Central, Exit F.

Just west of the Star Ferry Pier is the **International Finance Centre**, a business and shopping complex overlooking the Outer Islands Ferry Piers. The **IFC Mall** is one of the smartest and busiest in Central and the complex's **IFC2 Tower** reaches 420m high – even higher than the Peak Tram's upper terminus – and was Hong Kong's tallest building until the ICC tower in West Kowloon opened in 2010. Home to the Hong Kong Monetary Authority, IFC2's 88 floors are so well proportioned that its height

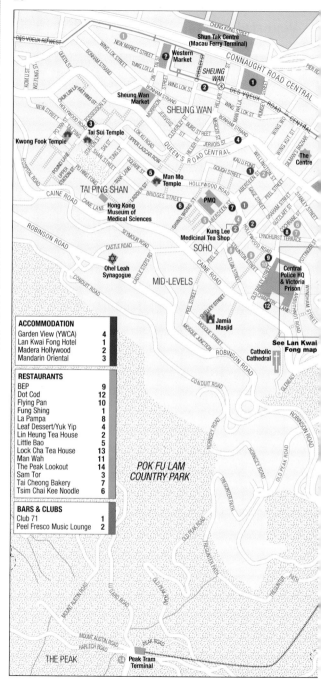

ACCOMMODATION

Garden View (YWCA)	4
Lan Kwai Fong Hotel	1
Madera Hollywood	2
Mandarin Oriental	3

RESTAURANTS

BEP	9
Dot Cod	12
Flying Pan	10
Fung Shing	1
La Pampa	8
Leaf Dessert/Yuk Yip	4
Lin Heung Tea House	2
Little Bao	5
Lock Cha Tea House	13
Man Wah	11
The Peak Lookout	14
Sam Tor	3
Tai Cheong Bakery	7
Tsim Chai Kee Noodle	6

BARS & CLUBS

Club 71	1
Peel Fresco Music Lounge	2

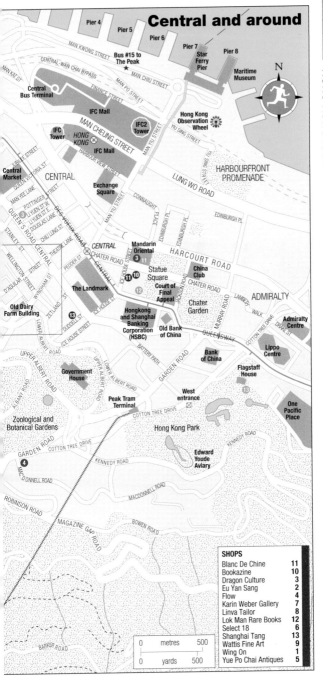

Central and around

SHOPS

Blanc De Chine	11
Bookazine	10
Dragon Culture	3
Eu Yan Sang	2
Flow	4
Karin Weber Gallery	7
Linva Tailor	8
Lok Man Rare Books	12
Select 18	6
Shanghai Tang	13
Wattis Fine Art	9
Wing On	1
Yue Po Chai Antiques	5

Hong Kong: an Opium War trophy

During the early nineteenth century, Britain – then a rising manufacturing and maritime power – faced a frustrating trade imbalance. British merchants were paying a fortune in silver every year for Chinese tea, silk and porcelain, but couldn't convince the Chinese to buy any British wares in return. So, the British began importing cheap opium from their holdings in India, flooding the Chinese market and causing a surge in addiction and demand. In 1839, alarmed at the Imperial court's rapidly-draining reserves of silver, Chinese officials stepped in to stop the trade – and Britain declared war to keep it going. After two years of British warships pounding Chinese ports with "gunboat diplomacy", in 1842 the Qing court was forced to sign the Treaty of Nanking, which – amongst other things – ceded Hong Kong island to Britain "in perpetuity".

is disguised until you consciously measure it against adjacent structures, or see its upper storeys hidden by cloud. Sadly, the tower is closed to the public.

Inland from the International Finance Centre are the three pastel-pink, marble and glass towers of Hong Kong's **Stock Exchange**, sprouting from Swiss architect Remo Riva's **Exchange Square**. The adjacent piazza has sculptures by Henry Moore and Elizabeth

Frink, while the interior is entirely computer-operated: the buildings' environment is electronically controlled, and the brokers whisk between floors in state-of-the-art talking elevators.

Statue Square

MAP P.28, POCKET MAP E6
Ⓜ Central, Exit K.

Statue Square, the heart of the late-nineteenth-century colony, is now uncomfortably bisected by Chater Road. The northern segment is bounded to the east by the members-only **Hong Kong Club**, housed inside a modern, bow-fronted tower; this is faced by the **Mandarin Oriental Hotel**, which hides an opulent interior inside a dull, box-like casing.

Across Chater Road, the southern half of Statue Square was once full of sculptures of the colony's founders and leaders, though only one remains: that of **Sir Thomas Jackson**, a nineteenth-century manager of the Hongkong and Shanghai Bank. This area is a meeting point for the territory's two hundred thousand Filipina *amahs*, or maids, who descend en masse on Central each Sunday to sociably picnic, shop, read, sing and have their hair cut. Filipinos comprise the largest non-Chinese population

Statue Square

Statue Square

Mandarin Oriental Hotel

in Hong Kong, alongside growing numbers of Indonesians, and minority groups of European, Indian and Pakistani descent.

The impressive, colonial-style granite structure with dome and colonnades on Statue Square's eastern side is the former Supreme Court, built in 1898, which until 2013 housed **LEGCO**, Hong Kong's governing Legislative Council. This was Hong Kong's nearest equivalent to a parliamentary building, but after the council relocated east to Wan Chai, the building reverted to its previous function, and today houses the Court of Final Appeal.

Three banks

MAP P.28, POCKET MAP E6
Ⓜ Central, Exit K.

Crossing the southern half of Statue Square and the busy Des Voeux Road puts you right underneath Sir Norman Foster's **Hongkong and Shanghai Banking Corporation (HSBC)** headquarters, which opened in 1986. The whole battleship-grey building is supported on eight groups of giant pillars and it's possible to walk right under the bank and come out on the other side – a necessity stipulated by the *feng shui* belief that the old centre of power on the island, Government House, should be accessible in a straight line by foot from the Star Ferry. You look up through the glass underbelly into a 60m-high atrium, with floors suspended from coathanger-like structures and linked by long

Elevated walkways

Many of the buildings in and around Central are linked together by a web of **elevated walkways**, a useful escape from the overwhelming crowds at street level – if you can navigate your way through connecting buildings. Using these it's just about possible to walk between Sheung Wan, Central, the Star Ferry Terminal and Wan Chai without touching the ground.

escalators that ride through each storey, and open offices ranged around the central atrium. The public banking facilities are on the first two floors, so you can ride the first couple of escalators from street level to have a look. The bronze lions at the front, named **Stephen** and **Stitt** after former HSBC directors, date back to the 1930s – one is still scarred from World War II shrapnel.

Across Garden Road to the east, I.M. Pei's 315m-high **Bank of China** is an angular, dark-glass building which towers over the HSBC building by 145m, its sharp edges designed to metaphorically "cut" into its nearby rival in a demonstration of aggressive *feng shui* (see page 34). Similarly, the BOC's knife-like profile stabs skywards like a *feng shui* antenna, to draw down good luck from the heavens before any can reach its shorter competitors.

Next to the HSBC, the **Old Bank of China** still stands, a diminutive but solid stone structure dating from 1950, which looks like a fossilized ancestor of its modern incarnation. It's now occupied by the **China Club**, a wealthy, members-only haven.

Queen's Road and Des Voeux Road

MAP P.28, POCKET MAP A4–D6
Ⓜ Central, Exits B, C & D

Queen's Road has been Central's main street since the 1840s, when, prior to land reclamation, it was on the waterfront. Running south from it, just west of HSBC, Duddell Street is home to **Shanghai Tang** (see page 42), one of Hong Kong's most recognisable brands, featuring designer clothing that blends traditional Chinese hems with pop art colours and designs.

Parallel to Duddell Street, **Ice House Street** was named after a

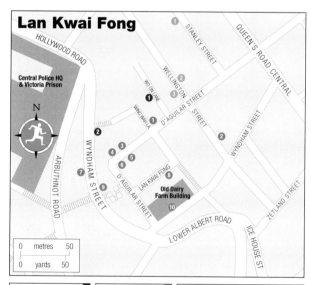

Lan Kwai Fong

SHOPS		RESTAURANTS		BARS & CLUBS			
Mountain Folkcraft	1	Luk Yu Tea House	1	Bit Point	4	Insomnia	6
Teresa Coleman	2	Tsui Wah	2	Club Qing	8	Keg Sports Bar	5
		Yung Kee	3	Dragon-i	7	Magnum Club	2
				Fringe Club	10	Origin	9
				Havana Bar	1	Volar	3

Des Voeux Road

building that once stored blocks of imported ice for use in the colony's early hospitals; following it uphill brings you onto Lower Albert Road, where the early twentieth-century **Old Dairy Farm Building**, in brown-and-cream brick, today houses the *Fringe Club* (see page 46) and the Foreign Correspondents' Club, a retreat for journalists, diplomats and lawyers.

Running west, Queen's Road and parallel **Des Voeux Road** (with its tramway) take in some of the territory's most exclusive shops and malls. These include **The Landmark** shopping complex, on the corner of Pedder Street and Des Voeux Road, which boasts a fountain in its atrium and is a key hub in the **pedestrian walkway** system that links all of Central's major buildings.

Whether you follow Queen's Road or Des Voeux Road west from here, look out for the parallel alleys which run between the two, **Li Yuen Street East** and **Li Yuen Street West**; both are packed tight with stalls selling women's clothes, silkwear, children's clothes, fabrics, imitation handbags and accessories.

Southwest of these alleys, over Queen's Road, **Pottinger Street**'s steps are similarly clogged with stalls selling ribbons, flowers, locks and other minor items.

Just west of Central Market, at 99 Queen's Road Central, is **The Centre**, designed by architect Denis Lau, and by night one of the most eye-catching features of the island's skyline. The building's horizontal bars of light change colour constantly and perform a dancing light show nightly at 8pm, best seen from The Peak or the Kowloon waterfront.

Lan Kwai Fong

MAP P.32, POCKET MAP B7
Ⓜ Central, Exit D.

The network of streets south of Queen's Road contains a burgeoning array of trendy pubs, bars, restaurants and clubs, at the heart of which is a sloping L-shaped lane whose name, **Lan Kwai Fong**, is now used to refer to the whole area. The entertainment kicks off mid-afternoon, with many places remaining open until dawn. Lan Kwai Fong is mostly frequented by expats and Chinese yuppies

Feng shui

Whatever the scale of a building project, the Chinese consider divination using **feng shui** (literally "wind and water") an essential part of the initial preparations. Reflecting Taoist cosmology, *feng shui* assesses how buildings must be positioned so as not to disturb the spiritual attributes of the surrounding landscape, which in a city naturally includes other buildings. Structures must be favourably orientated according to points on the compass and protected from local "unlucky directions" (features that drain or block the flow of good fortune) by other buildings, walls, hills, mountain ranges or water. It's not difficult to spot smaller manifestations of *feng shui* around buildings in Hong Kong, such as mirrors hung above doors or woks placed outside windows to deflect bad influences. Water features create positive *feng shui* (it is believed that wealth is borne along by the water), hence the price of harbour-view real estate.

– a good district to meet young, aspiring locals.

The Zoological and Botanical Gardens

MAP P.28, POCKET MAP D7
Entrances on Glenealy St and Albany Rd
Ⓜ Central, Exit K. Ⓦ lcsd.gov.hk. Daily
6am–7pm. Free.

Perching on the slopes south of Upper Albert Road, overlooking Central, are the low-key **Zoological and Botanical Gardens**, which opened in 1864. The **gateway and lions** at the main entrance commemorate Chinese soldiers who died defending Hong Kong in the 1940s; once inside, there's a nice mix of shrubs, trees and paved paths, with close-ups of the upper storeys of the Bank of China Tower and HSBC, but the main draw is the **aviaries**, home to rare cranes, songbirds and wildfowl. West across Albany Road (via an underpass) is a collection of primates, including lemurs, gibbons and orangutans.

Government House

MAP P.28, POCKET MAP D7
Upper Albert Rd Ⓜ Central, Exit K. Gardens and parts of the house open annually; dates announced in the local press. Free.
Government House was the residence of Hong Kong's colonial

governors from 1855 until the SAR's return to China in 1997. Hong Kong's current Chief Executive, CY Leung, has also taken up residence here despite the building's colonial associations and notoriously bad *feng shui* – made worse, no doubt, by the Bank of China (see page 34). The house is a strange blend of styles (the turret was added by the Japanese during World War II, when the building served as their military headquarters), and the gardens are notable for their rhododendrons, azaleas and a huge fishpond.

Hong Kong Park

MAP P.28, POCKET MAP E7
Ⓜ Admiralty, Exit C1. Ⓦ lcsd.gov.hk. Daily 6am–11pm. Free. Two-hour birdwatching tour meets near the west entrance Wed 8am (free; ☎ 2521 5059).

South from the Bank of China across Cotton Tree Drive, **Hong Kong Park** is beautifully landscaped in tiers up the hillside, though tackling all the steps is tough going in hot weather. Among the trees and boulders are ornamental lakes and waterfalls stocked with turtles and pelicans, alongside which a continual procession of brides pose for wedding photographs. Specific sights include a **conservatory** with dry and humid habitats for its orchids, cacti and trees, and the superb **Edward Youde Aviary** (daily 9am–5pm; free), an enormous, walk-through mesh tent, covering a piece of semi-tropical forest, home to some six hundred tropical birds. Despite their bright plumage, many of the resident species of parrots, waterfowl, forest pigeons and flycatchers can be surprisingly hard to spot, even with wooden walkways at branch height. A separate walkway just outside the top of the aviary passes between cages of endangered hornbills, whose massive hooked beaks were once fashioned into belt buckles by the Chinese aristocracy.

At the northern corner of Hong Kong Park is the elegantly colonial **Flagstaff House**, built in 1844 as the office and residence of the Commander of the British Forces in Hong Kong. Today, it stands in defiance of the surrounding skyscrapers, its cool white walls, shutters, high ceilings and polished wooden floors the epitome of understated colonial charm. It houses a fine collection of traditional Chinese teapots, cups and tea-making paraphernalia as the **Museum of Teaware** (daily except Tues 10am–6pm; free), documenting China's two-thousand-year love affair with tea drinking, and how the process has changed with time. You can sample different brews next door at the atmospheric **Lock Cha Tea House** (see page 44) inside the K.S. Lo Gallery, then browse the gallery's collection of seal stones – elegantly carved personal name stamps used by the Chinese in the old days to sign official documents.

The Lippo Centre

MAP P.28, POCKET MAP F6
Queensway Ⓜ Admiralty, Exit B.

The Lippo Centre is an eye-catching, segmented structure of mirrored glass designed by American architect Paul Rudolph for Australian millionaire Allan Bond in 1998. Supported on huge grey pillars, interlocking steel and glass spurs trace their way up the centre's twin hexagonal towers, creating an unmistakable landmark

Hong Kong Park & the Lippo Centre

The Peak

– though there's nothing of interest inside.

The Peak

MAP P.28, POCKET MAP B9

Peak Tram from Garden Rd (daily 7am–midnight, every 10–15min; $40 return, $28 one-way). Bus #15 from Exchange Square (daily 7am–12.30am, every 15min; $9.80; after 9am also from near Outer Island Pier 5). ⓦ hk-victoria-peak.com.

The wooded, 552m heights of **The Peak** – officially Victoria Peak – give you the only perspective that matters in Hong Kong: downwards, over Central and the magnificent harbour. Property up here, always favoured for being an escape from the high summer temperatures at sea level, has become the astronomically expensive prerogative of the colony's elite: residents include politicians, bank CEOs, various consul-generals and assorted celebrities.

The best way to ascend is aboard the **Peak Tram**, a 1.4km-long funicular railway, in operation since 1888. The eight-minute ascent tackles 27-degree slopes, forcing you back into your wooden bench as the carriages are steadily hauled

through the forest. The ride begins at the terminal on Garden Road and finishes at the **Peak Tower**, an ugly concrete structure generally referred to as the Flying Wok. Its sole virtue is the superb views from the Sky Terrace – which they charge a further $50 to access – encompassing the harbour, Tsim Sha Tsui's land reclamation projects and low-tech concrete tower blocks, right into the New Territories.

Free vistas can be savoured from the lookout 100m past the tower, or across the road, from the upper terrace of the **Peak Galleria**, a touristy complex full of shops and restaurants. It's a panorama that's difficult to tire of – come up again at night when the lights of Hong Kong transform the city into a glittering box of tricks.

You're not yet at the top of The Peak itself: four roads pan out from the tower, one of which, **Mount Austin Road**, provides a stiff twenty-minute walk up to **Victoria Peak Garden**. Alternatively, a **circuit** of The Peak via shady **Harlech Road** takes around an hour. First views are of Aberdeen and Lamma; later, as you turn into Lugard Road, Kowloon and Central come into sight. You can also **walk back to Central** from The Peak Tower in around forty minutes, via the **Old Peak Road**, a surfaced but steep track which descends through the forest and past Central's uppermost apartments, to emerge onto Robinson Road near the zoo.

Hollywood Road

MAP P.28, POCKET MAP B5–C6

ⓜ Central, Exit D2/Sheung Wan, Exit A2.
Hollywood Road, and the streets nearby, form a run of antique shops and, increasingly, art galleries – most charging collectors' prices. At the eastern end, it's hard to miss the former **Central Police Headquarters** at number 10 – known locally as Tai Kwun, or "Big Station" – with its overbearing

Art Deco facade, dated to 1919. Up the hill behind, a high stone wall encloses the old Victoria Prison, dating in part back to 1860s. Closed for over a decade, the whole complex is currently being converted into an "integrated space for history, culture and arts", which will feature stylish modern architecture alongside preserved older structures.

Moving west, check out the old-style **Kung Lee Medicinal Tea Shop** (公利真料竹蔗水) at the corner with Peel Street, which dates to the 1940s; if you can't take bitter tea, try freshly-squeezed sugarcane juice instead. Detouring south, **PMQ** (39 Aberdeen St ⓦ Sheung Wan exit A2 ☎ 2870 2335, ⓦ pmq. org.hk. Studios daily 1–8pm.), the former "Police Married Quarters", has now been converted into seven floors of artist/designer galleries and workshops rising around a central courtyard; a good venue, but yet to find its feet.

Just downhill from the Man Mo Temple (see below), **Upper Lascar Row** is a narrow street lined with antique and curio stalls, where it's still possible to unearth an inexpensive, low-key antique souvenir – even if most of the items on sale are reproductions (whatever stallholders might claim).

Man Mo Temple

MAP P.28, POCKET MAP C5
Hollywood Rd ⓦ Sheung Wan, Exit A2. Daily 8am–6pm. Free.

The **Man Mo Temple** is one of Hong Kong's oldest, built in the 1840s and equipped with decorations from mainland China, all hung with smouldering incense spirals. The temple's name derives from the words for "civil" (*man*) and "martial" (*mo*): the first attribute belongs to the god of literature, Man Cheong, who protects civil servants (he's the red-robed statue wielding a writing brush); the latter to the martial

Tai Ping Shan

Back in the 1860s, the **Tai Ping Shan** district was infamous for its plague-infested brothels and drinking dens, the haunt of low-life pirates and criminals. Today it's mostly memorable for the tough slog up **Ladder Street**, a steeply-stepped footpath climbing for 300m between the Man Mo and Caine Road. About halfway up Ladder Street, it's worth detouring west along **Tai Ping Shan Street** for a couple of unusual places of worship. The Kwong Fook Temple on the corner of Station Street, open-sided and roofed in corrugated sheeting, was founded in the 1850s by Chinese migrant workers, and is something of an ancestral shrine to those workers who died here, far from home. A little further along at the corner with Pound Lane, the Tai Sui Temple is dedicated to Duo Mou, the Taoist "Mother of Heaven", and the Sixty Tai Sui deities, each of whom represents a year in the Chinese astrological cycle.

Back on Ladder Street, keep climbing to the **Hong Kong Museum of Medical Sciences** (2 Caine Lane; ⓦ Sai Yun Ping ☎ 2549 5123, ⓦ hkmms.org.hk. Tues–Sat 10am–5pm, Sun 1–5pm; $20). To be honest, the red-brick Edwardian-era colonial building outshines the dusty cases of lab equipment inside, but this is also where French researcher Alexandre Yersin discovered, in 1894, that the bubonic plague virus was spread between animals and people by fleas.

deity, Kuan Ti (represented by another statue, in green, holding a sword). Kuan Ti is based on the real-life warrior Kuan Yu of the Three Kingdoms Period (around 220 AD), who is protector of pawnshops, policemen, secret societies and the military.

Sheung Wan

MAP P.28, POCKET MAP C5
ⓜ Sheung Wan.

Sheung Wan begins pretty much west of Jubilee Street, and though modern development has torn out many of the **old lanes** and their street vendors, a few – such as Wing Kut Street and Man Wa Lane – survive, and are full of stalls hawking calligraphy brushes, clothes and carved name stamps, or "chops". Sheung Wan's most distinctive structure is the **Shun Tak Centre**; set on the waterfront on Connaught Road, its twin towers are encased in a distinctive red framework and house the Macau Ferry Terminal. Opposite is the **Western Market** (daily 10am–7pm), whose fine Edwardian brick and ironwork shell houses two floors of fabric shops. For a modern, multi-storey Chinese produce market – involving vast amounts of fruit, vegetables and freshly slaughtered meat – try **Sheung Wan Market** on Morrison Street; the second floor is a mass of stalls (daily 6am–2am) serving all sorts of light meals.

The streets due west of here provide glimpses of the trades and industries that date back to Hong Kong's settlement. Many shops on Wing Lok Street and Bonham Strand specialize in **bird's nest** and **ginseng**. The nests are used to make bird's nest soup, a gastronomic speciality said to promote longevity; as the nest is tasteless, however, the dish's quality rests in the soup itself.

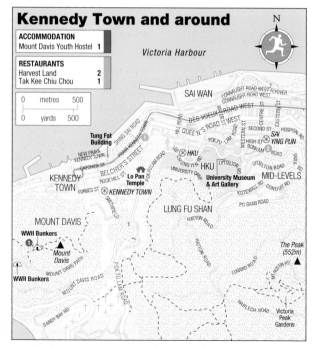

Kennedy Town and around

ACCOMMODATION	
Mount Davis Youth Hostel	1

RESTAURANTS	
Harvest Land	2
Tak Kee Chiu Chou	1

The Mid-Levels Escalator

The **Mid-Levels Escalator** cuts up the hillside for 800m from the footbridge across Queen's Road by the corner of Jubilee Street, via Hollywood Road and the popular restaurant district of **Soho**, ending at Conduit Road. It carries thirty thousand commuters daily on a one-way system, which runs uphill from 10.20am to midnight, and downhill from 6am to 10am (use accompanying staircases to go against the flow). All told, it's a twenty-minute ride from bottom to top, or 45 minutes if you have to walk.

Ginseng, the root of a plant found in Southeast Asia and North America, is prescribed for a whole host of problems, from reviving mental faculties in the aged, to curing impotence – some of the larger ginseng trading companies have venerable interiors decked out in teak and glass panels. Many shops in Ko Shing Street are dedicated wholesalers, selling **traditional Chinese medicines** such as deer antlers, crushed pearls, dried seahorses and assorted herbalists' paraphernalia. Others lean towards kitchen supplies with their piles of dried mushrooms, salted and preserved fish, dried squid, oysters, sea slugs, scallops and seaweed.

University Museum and Art Gallery

MAP P.38

Fung Ping Shan building, 90 Bonham Rd Ⓜ HKU exit A1 ☎ 2241 5500 Ⓦ umag.hku.hk. Mon–Sat 9.30am–6pm, Sun 1–6pm. Free.

Aside from representative cases of antique Chinese pottery, calligraphy, and bronzes, this museum is best known for its **woodwork**, from temple statues to domestic furniture and elaborately carved screens, and an unusual collection of 966 **Nestorian crosses** from the Yuan dynasty (1271–

Mid-Levels Escalator

Tung Fat building

1368), associated with the Syrian Christian church of the time, which had sent envoys to China.

Kennedy Town

MAP P.38

Ⓜ Kennedy Town.

Terminus for both the tram and MTR from Central, **Kennedy Town** is a slightly shabby grid of small businesses and residential blocks (including a few remaining **tong lau** buildings). It's an easy taste of ordinary Hong Kong, and with views from the waterfront taking in the western mouth of Victoria Harbour, there's a definite maritime feel to the place.

For the town's one sight, head up steep steps from Belcher's Street to the small **Lo Pan Temple** on Ching Ling Terrace (daily 8am–5pm). There's a roofline decorated in bright porcelain dragons, fish and lions, and a plain interior with a shrine to Lo Pan, the patron deity of carpenters; his birthday is celebrated here by construction workers every thirteenth of the sixth lunar month.

Mount Davis

MAP P.38

Ⓜ Kennedy Town.

Immediately west of Kennedy Town, **Mount Davis** (269m) is chiefly of interest for its youth hostel (see page 126); most people catch a taxi up.

A short way past the hostel, Mount Davis' level **summit** sports a picnic area and a network of overgrown concrete bunkers – part of a chain of gun batteries designed to defend the harbour, before Hong Kong fell to the Japanese in December 1941. There are good views over the western side of the island from here, while the bunkers are popular with war game enthusiasts.

Tong Lau

Hong Kong's classic post-war apartment building, with distinctive rounded, overhanging upper floors and long bands of windows, *tong lau* are becoming a rare sight today, as whole districts of them are torn down and replaced by modern high-rises. One exception is Kennedy Town's **Tung Fat building**, at the corner of New Praya and North Street, which has been elegantly modernised in a way the original designers would have approved, keeping all the distinctive *tong lau* features.

Shops

Blanc De Chine

MAP P.28, POCKET MAP E6
Shop 123, Landmark Building, Central
Ⓜ Central, Exit K. Mon–Sat 10.30am–
7.30pm, Sun noon–6pm.

Elegant and expensive designs for
men and women loosely based on
traditional Chinese clothes, mostly
in silk or cashmere.

Bookazine

MAP P.28, POCKET MAP E6
Prince's Building, 10 Chater Rd Ⓜ Central,
Exit K. Mon–Sat 9.30am–7.30pm. Sun
10am–7pm.

Bookshop with a large collection
on Hong Kong and China, from
glossy coffee-table works to novels,
local maps and hiking guides.

Dragon Culture

MAP P.28, POCKET MAP B5
231 Hollywood Rd, Sheung Wan Ⓜ Sheung
Wan, Exit A2. ☎ 2545 8098. Mon–Sat
10.30am–6pm.

Upmarket Chinese antiques,
including pottery, porcelain and
bronzeware; a good place to find
museum-quality artefacts.

Eu Yan Sang

MAP P.28, POCKET MAP C5
Shum Tower, 268 Des Voeux Rd, Central
Ⓜ Sheung Wan, Exit A1. Daily 9am–7.30pm.

Hong Kong's most famous
medicine shop, founded in 1879,
and now with branches across
Southeast Asia. A source of teas,
herbs and Chinese medicines, all
carefully weighed and measured.

Flow

MAP P.28, POCKET MAP C5
Kai Fung Mansion, 189–205 Queen's Road
Central. Ⓜ Sheung Wan, Exit E2. Daily
noon–7pm.

The city's best secondhand
bookshop, full of everything from
holiday pulp to coffee-table albums
and DVDs. Takes time to sort
through the crowded shelves.

Karin Weber Gallery

MAP P.28, POCKET MAP C5
20 Aberdeen St, Central Ⓜ Sheung Wan,
Exit A2. Ⓦ karinwebergallery.com. Tues–
Sat 11am–7pm.

Large selection of mid-price
contemporary fine art and regular
pieces of antique furniture; they
also organize furniture-buying trips
to warehouses on the mainland.

Linva Tailor

MAP P.28, POCKET MAP C6
38 Cochrane St, Central Ⓜ Central, Exit D2.

Well-established ladies' tailor
famous for its 1950s-style
cheongsams – they provided the
wardrobe for the stylish, moody
Hong Kong romance, *In the Mood
for Love*.

Lok Man Rare Books

MAP P.28, POCKET MAP C6
6 Chancery Lane. Ⓜ Central, Exit D1. ☎
2868 1056, Ⓦ lokmanbooks.com. Tues–Sat
11am–7pm.

A step back in time, to an era
of peaceful browsing, wooden
bookshelves, and the scent of antique
leather bindings. Particularly strong
on travel and exploration but expect
eyewatering prices.

Blanc De Chine

Mountain Folkcraft

MAP P.32, POCKET MAP B7

12 Wo On Lane Ⓜ Central, Exit D ☎ 2523 2817, ⓦ mountainfolkcraft.com. Mon–Sat 10am–6.30pm.

All kinds of Chinese folk art, including beautifully embroidered jackets from the Miao ethnic minority, but really excels in traditional, woodblock-printed *nianhua*, colourful good-luck pictures pasted up for the Chinese New Year.

Select 18

MAP P.28, POCKET MAP C5

18 Bridges Street Ⓜ Sheung Wan, Exit A2. ☎ 2549 2589.

Vintage clothing, spectacles, vinyl and melange of interesting old-time bric-a-brac (enamel thermos flasks, cine gear, typewriters, photos), mostly sourced from Hong Kong.

Shanghai Tang

MAP P.28, POCKET MAP D6

1 Duddell St, Central Ⓜ Central, Exit D2. ⓦ shanghaitang.com. Daily 10.30am–8pm.

Beautifully done up in 1930s Shanghai style, this store specializes in new versions of traditional Chinese clothing – often in their trademark combination of pink, green and black silk – and they also offer a made-to-order service. It's expensive, but the good, and regular, sales are definitely worth a look.

Teresa Coleman

MAP P.32, POCKET MAP A6

55 Wyndham St, Soho Ⓜ Central, Exit D2. ☎ 2526 2450 (call for appointment).

Specialist in antique textiles, including Tibetan rugs and thangkas, Chinese silk robes and ethnic embroideries.

Wattis Fine Art

MAP P.28, POCKET MAP C6

20 Hollywood Rd, Central Ⓜ Central, Exit D2. Mon–Sat 10am–6pm.

An intriguing cave, full of China-related old maps, paintings and prints. Don't expect bargains – these are collector's prices – but it's a fascinating place for a browse.

Wing On

MAP P.28, POCKET MAP C5

211 Des Voeux Rd Ⓜ Sheung Wan, Exit A1. Daily 9am–6pm.

Long-established Chinese department store selling standard day-to-day goods.

Mountain Folkcraft

Yue Po Chai Antiques

MAP P.28, POCKET MAP B5

132–134 Hollywood Rd, Central Ⓜ Sheung
Wan, Exit A2 ☎ 2540 4374.

Browse through this maze of dusty
pots, jars, plates and ephemera,
and, among good-looking
reproductions, you'll find some
genuine antiques.

Restaurants

BEP

MAP P.28, POCKET MAP C6

88–90 Wellington St, Ⓜ Central, Exit D2. ☎
2581 9992, Ⓦ bep.hk. Daily 11.30am–
4.30pm & 6–11pm.

Excellent Vietnamese food,
cramped seating and unusually
good service for Hong Kong. The
tomato and crab soup, *pho* and *rau
cuon* rolls are the dishes of choice.
$100 a head.

Dot Cod

MAP P.28, POCKET MAP E6

Basement, Prince's Building, 10 Chater
Rd, Central Ⓜ Central, Exit K ☎ 2810 6988.
Mon–Sat 7.30am–11.30pm.

A chic, pricey place to eat fairly
straightforward British-style
seafood – rock oysters, fish and
chips, scallops and char-grilled
sardines. They do good breakfasts
too. Set lunch $298.

Flying Pan

MAP P.28, POCKET MAP C6

9 Old Bailey St, Soho Ⓜ Central, Exit D2
☎ 2140 6333, Ⓦ the-flying-pan.com.
Daily, 24hr.

All-day breakfast fry-ups for around
$100, with generous portions of
almost unlimited combinations
of eggs, bacon, burgers, beans,
sausages, tomatoes and mushrooms.
Their coffee isn't the best, but it's a
great place to start the day.

Fung Shing (鳳城酒家)

MAP P.28, POCKET MAP B4

G/F, Sea View Commercial Building,
21–24 Connaught Road West, Sheung Wan.
Ⓜ Sheung Wan, Exit B ☎ 2815 8689. Daily

BEP

7am–4pm & 6–11pm.

Signed in Chinese, this friendly
place serves excellent, inexpensive
Shunde-style *dim sum* – try honey-
roast pork or paper-thin *sheung fan*.

Harvest Land

MAP P.38, POCKET MAP A5

Kam Ning Mansion, 13–15 Bonham Rd. Ⓜ
Sai Ying Pun, Exit C. ☎ 2385 2382. Daily
7am–10pm.

Friendly Hong Kong-style café
serving one-plate meals, including
local takes on spaghetti and
club sandwiches, plus Chinese
staples such as pork knuckle and
noodles. Lunch sets around $50,
including tea.

La Pampa

MAP P.28, POCKET MAP C6

32 Staunton St, Soho Ⓜ Central, Exit
D2 ☎ 2868 6959. Daily noon–2.30pm &
6–11pm.

Blow out on the finest Argentinian
steak, in upwards of 250g portions,
grilled to your instructions and
served with nominal quantities of
vegetables. $500 a head.

Leaf Dessert/Yuk Yip (玉葉甜品)

MAP P.28, POCKET MAP C6

2 Elgin Street, Central. Ⓜ Sheung Wan, Exit E1. Daily noon–12.30am.

Tiny hole-in-the-wall serving local-style desserts; somewhere to grab a sweet snack in passing, or to round off a light meal eaten elsewhere. Specialities include mung beans and kelp soup ($15), and *tangyuan* rice balls scattered with toasted sesame seeds and coconut ($16).

Lin Heung Tea House

MAP P.28, POCKET MAP C5

160–164 Wellington St, Sheung Wan Ⓜ Sheung Wan, Exit E1 ☎ 2544 4556. Daily 6am–11pm, dim sum served until 4pm.

This popular, inexpensive *dim sum* restaurant relocated here from Guangzhou (in China) around 1950, and they've been so busy since, they haven't had time to change the furnishings or allow their ancient staff to retire. Brusque atmosphere with plain, good food. Crowds queue up for their Mid-Autumn Festival mooncakes.

Little Bao

MAP P.28, POCKET MAP C6

66 Staunton St, Central (next to PMQ) Ⓜ Central Exit D2, Sheung Wan Exit A2. ☎ 2194 0202, Ⓦ little-bao.com. Mon–Fri 6–11pm, Sat noon–4pm & 6–11pm, Sun noon–4pm & 6–10pm.

Fun fast food based around chef May Chow's reinvention of Chinese stuffed buns (*bao*), here served more like burgers. Don't miss the truffle fries, spicy chicken drumstick or signature pork belly *bao* ($80).

Lock Cha Tea House

MAP P.28, POCKET MAP E7

K.C. Lo Gallery, Hong Kong Park, Central Ⓜ Admiralty, Exit C1 ☎ 2801 7177. Daily 10am–8pm, closed second Tues of the month.

Elegant place furnished with carved Chinese screens and wooden tables, serving vegetarian *dim sum* and specialist Chinese teas – all brewed and served differently. Aimed at tourists rather than locals, though excellent quality; expect to pay $150 a head.

Luk Yu Tea House

MAP P.28, POCKET MAP D6

24–26 Stanley St, just west of D'Aguilar St, Central Ⓜ Central, Exit D2 ☎ 2523 5464. Daily 7am–10pm.

A snapshot from the 1930s, with old wooden furniture and ceiling fans, this self-consciously traditional restaurant's mainstay is *dim sum*. Despite local fame, the food, though good quality, barely justifies its tourist-inflated prices or famously offhand service. Upwards of $200 a head.

Man Wah

MAP P.28, POCKET MAP E6

25/F, Hotel, 5 Connaught Rd Ⓜ Central, Exit A2 ☎ 2825 4003. Daily noon–2.30pm & 6.30–10pm.

Subtle and accomplished *dim sum* and southern Chinese food at connoisseurs' prices ($800 a head and up), though the stunning harbour views outperform the menu.

The Peak Lookout

MAP P.28, POCKET MAP B9

121 Peak Rd, The Peak ☎ 2849 1000. Mon–Thurs 10.30am–11.30pm, Fri & Sat 10.30am–1am, Sun 8.30am–11pm.

The stone colonial building with raked ceilings makes a nice setting for working your way through their Asian-Indian menu. Pricey, but reasonable value for brunch or alfresco night-time dining. Reckon on around $500 per head.

Sam Tor

MAP P.28, POCKET MAP D6

30 Pottinger St, Central Ⓜ Central, Exit D2 ☎ 2801 6352. Mon–Fri 9am–8pm, Sat 9am–6pm.

Originally famous for its "white cooked" goose innards (very crunchy; HK$60), many now opt for their wonton noodle soup (HK$28 a bowl). Get in before noon if you don't want to join the huge queue.

Tai Cheong Bakery

MAP P.28, POCKET MAP C6
35 Lyndhurst Terrace, Central ⓂCentral, Exit D2 ☏ 2544 3475. Daily 7.30am–9pm.
You wouldn't know it from the Chinese-only sign and basic tiled interior, but this tiny establishment was founded in 1954 and has since spawned a Hong Kong-wide chain. Best for Hong Kong-style egg tarts (not grilled like Macau's version; $6) and flaky *char siu* pastries ($9).

Tak Kee Chiu Chou (德記潮州菜館)

MAP P.38, POCKET MAP A6
3 Belcher's Street, Kennedy Town. Ⓜ Kennedy Town, Exit B. ☏ 2819 5568. Tues–Sun 11.30am–3pm & 5.30–11pm.
Popular restaurant specialising in dishes from the southern Chinese town of Chaozhou: steamed fish, roast goose, oyster omelette, crisp-skinned sausage, and stewed pork belly with preserved greens. Expect to wait for a table. Mains around $70.

Tsim Chai Kee Noodle

MAP P.28, POCKET MAP D6
98 Wellington St, Central Ⓜ Central, Exit D2

☏ 2850 6471. Daily 9am–10pm.
This place is easily located by the lunchtime queue tailing downhill. It's definitely worth the wait, and even worth being jammed into the packed interior, for the famous wonton – jokingly known locally as "ping-pong wonton" because of their huge size – served in soup for just $29.

Tsui Wah

MAP P.32, POCKET MAP B6
17–19 Wellington St, Central Ⓜ Central, Exit D2 ☏ 2525 6338. Daily 24hr.
Multistorey institution serving a huge array of inexpensive Cantonese fast food (dishes about $60), but the fishball noodle soup is the thing to go for, along with Hai Nam chicken or the very sweet desserts. Extremely busy at lunchtimes.

Yung Kee

MAP P.32, POCKET MAP B6
32–40 Wellington St, Central Ⓜ Central, Exit D2 ☏ 2522 1624. Daily 11am–11.30pm.
A Hong Kong institution with a Michelin star, serving classic Cantonese food. Their roast pork and goose are superb, or try the set meals from $400.

Tsim Chai Kee Noodle

Yung Kee

Bars and clubs

Bit Point

MAP P.32, POCKET MAP A7
46–48 Wyndham St, Lan Kwai Fong
Ⓜ Central, Exit D2 ☎ 2523 7436. Mon–Fri
noon–2am, Sat & Sun 5pm–2am; happy
hour 4–9pm.
German theme bar serving meals
until around 10pm, after which
the bar starts selling industrial
quantities of lager and schnapps.

Club 71

MAP P.28, POCKET MAP C5
67 Hollywood Rd, Central Ⓜ Sheung Wan,
Exit A2 ☎ 2858 7071. Mon–Sat 5pm–1am.
This tiny, hard-to-find bohemian
place has a reasonably priced happy
hour and a front-of-house terrace.
Look for 69 Hollywood Road and
take Man Hing Lane around the
back. Watch out for the cat.

Club Qing

MAP P.32, POCKET MAP B7

10/F, Cosmos Building, 8–11 Lan Kwai
Fong, Central Ⓜ Central D2. ☎ 9379 7628,
Ⓦ clubqing.com. Mon–Sat 6pm–1am.
Smart bar specialising in Japanese
whisky (they claim to carry every
available variety) plus rare Scotch –
tasting sets are available. Also does
a good line in French wine, craft
beers and cocktails.

Dragon-i

MAP P.32, POCKET MAP A7
The Centrium, 60 Wyndham St, Central Ⓜ
Central D2. ☎ 3110 1222 Ⓦ dragon-i.com.
hk. Bar opens 5pm, club from 11.30pm.
Stylish Chinese restaurant by day,
all plush seating and red lanterns,
which metamorphoses into a
popular bar and house/hip-hop
club after dark – the Brazilian
music manager is former Arsenal
defender, Chris Samba.

Fringe Club

MAP P.32, POCKET MAP B7
2 Lower Albert Rd Ⓜ Central, Exit D2
☎ 2521 7251, Ⓦ hkfringeclub.com. Mon–

Thurs noon–midnight, Fri & Sat noon–3am; happy hour 4–9pm.

The ground-floor bar of this theatre and art-gallery complex has good-value beers and live music, and there's also a popular rooftop bar.

Havana Bar

MAP P.32, POCKET MAP B7

4/F, The Plaza, 21 D'Aguilar Street, Lan Kwai Fong Ⓜ Central, Exit D2 ☏ 2851 4880, Ⓦ havanabar.com.hk. Mon–Fri 6pm–12.30am, Sat 6pm–1am.

This popular bar offers a reprieve from Lan Kwai Fong's evening crowds, with a spacious terrace and the largest selection of rum in the city. Good tapas too.

Insomnia

MAP P.32, POCKET MAP A7

38–44 D'Aguilar St, Lan Kwai Fong Ⓜ Central, Exit D2 ☏ 2525 0957, 24hr; happy hour 8am–9pm.

Street-side bar where, early in the evening, conversation is possible. Later, the house band plays covers at full volume.

Keg sports bar

MAP P.32, POCKET MAP A7

52 D'Aguilar St Ⓜ Central, Exit D2 ☏ 2810 0369. Sun–Thurs 5pm–1am, Fri & Sat 5pm–2am.

Decked out in wood and metal trim to resemble the inside of a barrel, this place has a range of imported beers, including Molson, Boags and Cascade. Popular with expats.

Magnum Club

MAP P.32, POCKET MAP B7

1 Wellington St Ⓜ Central, Exit D2 ☏ 2116 1602, Ⓦ magnumclub.com.hk. Mon–Sat 10pm–2am.

Huge bar and DJ-driven dance venue on three floors (plus gold-plated bathrooms and an outdoor terrace), one of which is for VIPs only.

Origin

MAP P.32, POCKET MAP A7

G/F, 48 Wyndham St Ⓜ Central, Exit D2

☏ 2668 5583. Mon–Thurs 5pm–1am, Fri & Sat 5pm–2am.

Brick and exposed dark timber interior lend tropical ambiance to what is, essentially, a very stylish gin bar, serving Mother's Ruin in a bewildering variety of cocktails.

Peel Fresco Music Lounge

MAP P.28, POCKET MAP C6

49 Peel St, Central Ⓜ Sheung Wan Exit E1. ☏ 2540 2046, Ⓦ peel-fresco.com. Daily 7pm–2am.

Slightly outrageously claims to be Hong Kong's only true live music venue – though fair enough if you're looking for a dark, atmospheric, crowded jazz club. Hosts regular local talent, plus visiting bands.

Volar

MAP P.32, POCKET MAP A7

Basement 38–44 D'Aguillar St, Lan Kwai Fong Ⓜ Central Exit D2. ☏ 2810 1510 Ⓦ facebook.com/volarhongkong. Tues–Fri 7pm–5am, Sat 9pm–5am.

Long-established, chic dance club known for its star DJs and over-the-top sound system belting out r'n'b, hip-hop and electronica.

Origin

Hong Kong Island: Wan Chai, Causeway Bay and Happy Valley

Wan Chai and Causeway Bay stretch 4km east from Central along Hong Kong Island's north shore. With high-rises and congested expressways in all directions, this isn't a pretty area, though packed with eating, drinking and shopping opportunities. Wan Chai's enduring reputation for seedy bars was immortalized in Richard Mason's 1957 novel, *The World of Suzie Wong*, but the area has some architectural gems and even a semi-rural walk to offer. Further east, Causeway Bay is a lively spread of shops, parks and restaurants, though land reclamation has made a joke of the name – the only surviving maritime feature is a typhoon shelter. To the south, Happy Valley is worth a trip on Wednesday evenings to take in the atmosphere of the horse races – Hong Kong's only legal betting outlet.

The Convention and Exhibition Centre

MAP P.50, POCKET MAP H5–H6
Convention Avenue Ⓜ Wan Chai, Exit A1 Ⓦ hkcec.com.

The standout **Convention and Exhibition Centre**, whose distinctively flattened, curved roof juts out into the harbour, is where the British formally handed Hong Kong back to China in June 1997. As such, it's a huge draw with Chinese tourists, who come to pose beside the commemorative golden **Forever Blooming Bauhinia Sculpture** on the harbourside terrace here. If you like your fine art, it's worth checking the centre's event calendar to see if any of the big international **auction houses** are holding free previews of forthcoming lots.

Cross-harbour ferries from Tsim Sha Tsui's Star Ferry terminal (daily 7.30am–10.50pm; every 10–20min; $2.70) dock just east of the Exhibition Centre at the **Wan Chai Star Ferry Pier**.

Central Plaza

MAP P.50, POCKET MAP H6
Harbour Rd Ⓜ Wan Chai, Exit A1.

Sited opposite the Convention and Exhibition Centre, **Central Plaza** is another notable architectural marvel – it's the world's tallest building made of reinforced concrete (374m). Triangular in shape, it's topped by a glass pyramid from which a 64m mast protrudes: the locals dubbed it "The Big Syringe". It's lit at night by luminous neon panels, while the spire on top of the pyramid has four sections that change colour every fifteen minutes to show the time. There's a **public viewing bay** on the 46th floor (Mon–Fri 8am–8pm; free), which comprises a whole floor of giant windows where you can get a walk-around 360-degree view over the harbour and neighbouring buildings.

Queen's Road East

MAP P.50, POCKET MAP G7–K8
Ⓜ Admiralty, Exit J.

Inland, up against The Peak's foothills, **Queen's Road East** features a concentration of furniture stores, many offering fine-quality reproduction antique Chinese wooden chairs, screens and tables. Around halfway down, **Hung Shing Temple** occupies a natural grotto right on the roadside and is dedicated to a mix of Chinese gods, including Hung Shing himself, a deified Tang dynasty official who was able to forecast the weather. Nearby, the cylindrical Hopewell Centre is a useful landmark, overshadowing the tiny former **Wan Chai Post Office**, built in 1915.

Several side streets off Queen's Road East are worth a detour. Narrow **Tai Yuen Street** hosts a crowded outdoor market selling all manner of household goods, food, cheap clothing and toys; while **Lee Tung Street**, once famous for its hand printed greetings cards, has been reconstructed as an open-air mall, with all the usual upmarket boutiques (and some good restaurants) inside antique-style shopfronts. Further east, nondescript **Stone Nullah** **Lane** heads steeply uphill past the eye-catching **Blue House**, one of the last surviving examples of early twentieth-century "walkup" tenement buildings in Hong Kong. At the top of the lane, the splendid **Pak Tai Temple** (daily 8am–5pm) is crowned in decorative roof tiles, featuring operatically posed figures from Chinese folklore and mythology. Pak Tai, the Northern Emperor, is considered a guardian against flooding, and a bronze statue inside shows him overpowering evil forces in the shape of a turtle and snake.

Bowen Road and Lovers Rock

MAP P.50, POCKET MAP D8–K9
Ⓜ Wan Chai.

It's a stiff hike up lanes from beside the Old Wan Chai Post Office or Pak Tai Temple to **Bowen Road**, a level pedestrian path among the thick forest above Wan Chai, offering occasional glimpses of the city through the canopy. It's a popular spot with walkers and joggers, and is amazingly wild given its location just minutes from Wan Chai's busy expressways

Lovers Rock

Noon Day Gun

– watch out for snakes along the path. Walk east and you'll soon come to steps ascending to **Lovers Rock**, a huge stone boulder pointing rudely skywards above the trees, draped in festive red ribbons and a popular pilgrimage spot for young women during the annual Maidens' Festival.

The Noon Day Gun

MAP P.50, POCKET MAP L6
Gloucester Rd Ⓜ Causeway Bay, Exit D1.
Ever since colonial times, a ship's cannon known as the **Noon Day Gun** has been fired daily across the harbour at Wan Chai. Nobody seems to know why – there are several conflicting stories – and with mainland Chinese influence growing in Hong Kong, there's talk of the ceremony being discontinued. At any rate, unless you catch the actual event, the gun itself is underwhelming; get here via the subway from the car park next to the *Excelsior Hotel* opposite.

Victoria Park

MAP P.50, POCKET MAP M5–M6
Ⓜ Causeway Bay, Exit E. 24hr.

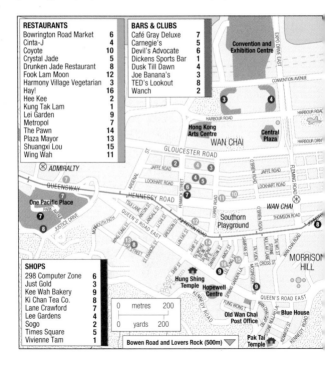

RESTAURANTS	
Bowrington Road Market	6
Cinta-J	4
Coyote	10
Crystal Jade	5
Drunken Jade Restaurant	8
Fook Lam Moon	12
Harmony Village Vegetarian	3
Hay!	16
Hee Kee	2
Kung Tak Lam	1
Lei Garden	9
Metropol	7
The Pawn	14
Plaza Mayor	13
Shuangxi Lou	15
Wing Wah	11

BARS & CLUBS	
Café Gray Deluxe	7
Carnegie's	5
Devil's Advocate	6
Dickens Sports Bar	1
Dusk Till Dawn	4
Joe Banana's	3
TED's Lookout	8
Wanch	2

SHOPS	
298 Computer Zone	6
Just Gold	3
Kee Wah Bakery	9
Ki Chan Tea Co.	8
Lane Crawford	7
Lee Gardens	4
Sogo	2
Times Square	5
Vivienne Tam	1

Sited east of Gloucester Road, **Victoria Park** is a flat, spacious spread of paving, sports fields and ornamental borders. It's busy around the clock, with martial arts practitioners and old men airing their caged songbirds at the crack of dawn, people cooling off on benches under the trees at midday, and football matches in the afternoon. A couple of times a year the park hosts some lively festivals, including a flower market at Chinese New Year, a lantern display for the Mid-Autumn Festival and the annual candlelit vigil for the victims of Tiananmen Square on June 4.

Times Square

MAP P.50, POCKET MAP K7
Ⓜ Causeway Bay, Exit A Ⓦ timessquare. com.hk.

The most startling fixture in the Causeway Bay shopping area is the beige blockbuster of a building that is **Times Square**, at the corner of Matheson and Russell streets. Spearing skywards, it exemplifies Hong Kong's modern architecture, where only vertical space is available and distinction is attained by unexpected design – in this case, a monolithic shopping mall supported by great marble trunks and featuring a cathedral window and giant video advertising screen. At ground level there's a cinema and direct access to the MTR; there are also plenty of pricey restaurants inside.

Happy Valley Racecourse

MAP P.50, POCKET MAP K8-L9
Ⓜ Causeway Bay Ⓦ hkjc.com.

Once a malarial swamp, initially settled, then abandoned, by the British, Happy Valley – or *pau ma dei* (horseracing track) in Cantonese – means one thing only to locals: gambling. All other forms of betting are banned in

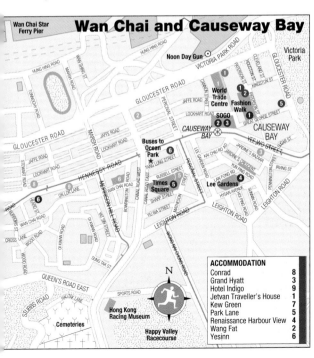

ACCOMMODATION	
Conrad	8
Grand Hyatt	3
Hotel Indigo	9
Jetvan Traveller's House	1
Kew Green	7
Park Lane	5
Renaissance Harbour View	4
Wang Fat	2
Yesinn	6

Hong Kong, and the **Happy Valley Racecourse** is the traditional centre of this multi-million-dollar business, with a second track at Sha Tin in the New Territories. It's controlled by the Hong Kong Jockey Club, one of the colony's power bastions since its foundation in 1884, with a board of stewards made up of the leading lights of Hong Kong big business. A percentage of the profits go to social and charitable causes – including funding for many hospitals – and such is the passion for betting in Hong Kong that the racing season pulls in over $80 billion per year.

The season runs from September to mid-June and there are usually meetings every Wednesday night, an intense experience with the crowds packed into the high stands surrounding the tight track. Entrance to the public enclosure is $10; there you can mix with a beery expat crowd, watch the horses being paraded before each race, and pump the staff to make sense of the intricate accumulator bets that Hong Kong bookies specialize in. Other options include joining the hard-bitten Chinese punters up in the stands, mostly watching the action on television ($20, plus all the cigarette smoke and Cantonese cursing you can handle), or signing up for a **Come Horseracing tour** (Ⓦ splendid. hk or Ⓦ grayline.com.hk; from $1100), which will take you to the course, feed you before the races, get you into the members' enclosure and provide some racing tips. You need to be over 18 and have been in Hong Kong for less than three weeks – take your passport to any HK tourist office at least a day before the race.

On the second floor of the main building at the racecourse, the **Hong Kong Racing Museum** (daily noon–7pm; free) presents various aspects of Hong Kong's racing history, from the early days in Happy Valley through to the various charitable projects funded by the Jockey Club. Racing buffs can also study champion racehorse characteristics and famous jockeys in the museum's eight galleries and cinema.

The Cemeteries

MAP P.50, POCKET MAP J8–K9
Wong Nai Chung Rd Ⓦ Causeway Bay. Daily 7am–6pm. Free.

The Cemeteries

Museum of Coastal Defence

The series of terraced hillside **cemeteries** west of the racecourse provides an interesting snapshot of the territory's ethnic and religious mix during its earliest days, with separate enclosures for Muslim, Catholic, Protestant, Parsee and Jewish inhabitants. The large Protestant cemetery is probably the most interesting, full of shady fig trees and grandiose granite monuments dating back to the 1850s, and a bit wild and overgrown towards the corners. It's noteworthy that just about everyone buried here before the 1950s seems to have died prematurely, often in virulent epidemics – probably because fewer expatriates lived permanently in Hong Kong before this time, and would have returned home after retiring.

Museum of Coastal Defence

MAP P.50, POCKET MAP L5
Ⓜ Shau Kei Wan/tram or bus #2 from Central to Shau Kei Wan, then a signed 1km walk along Shau Kei Wan Main St. ☎ 2569 1500, Ⓦ hk.coastaldefence.museum. Daily except Thurs 10am–5pm. $10, free on Wed.

Actually some way east from Causeway Bay, the **Museum of Coastal Defence** occupies the site of the Lei Yue Mun Fort, built by the British in 1887 to defend Victoria Harbour. Set high up on a hillside overlooking **Lei Yue Mun** – the "Carp Gate", Victoria Harbour's narrowest point – the bulk of the museum is in the renovated redoubt, the exhibition rooms reached by a maze of brick tunnels. The museum covers all stages of Hong Kong's maritime history, and exhibits include an opium-pipe display, moving letters from prisoners of war under the Japanese, and the richly embroidered satin army uniforms of Ming and Qing dynasty soldiers, studded with iron rivets. It's all fascinating, but also – unless you have a special interest in military history – probably a bit overwhelming. Outside, accompanied by stunning views of the rugged eastern end of Victoria Harbour, there's a marked trail past restored gun emplacements, underground magazines, a torpedo station and a gunpowder factory.

Shops

298 Computer Zone

MAP P.50, POCKET MAP J7
298 Hennessy Rd, Wan Chai Ⓜ Wan Chai,
Exit A4.

Despite the massive sign outside,
it's hard to find the entrance to this
warren-like place, full of booths
selling smart-phone, gaming and
computer gear on three levels.
Reasonably priced accessories
and software, though hardware is
expensive.

Just Gold

MAP P.50, POCKET MAP L6
SOGO, Hennessy Rd, Wan Chai Ⓜ Causeway
Bay, Exit D.

Local chain specializing in fun,
fashionable, cheapish jewellery
designs for young women.

Kee Wah Bakery (奇華餅家)

MAP P.50, POCKET MAP H8
188 Queen's Road East Ⓜ Wan Chai Exit
A5. ☎ 2785 6066. Daily 7.30am–7pm.

Founded in 1936, and housed
inside a period-style building at
the end of Lee Tung Avenue, this

Kee Wah Bakery

Ki Chan Tea Co.

MAP P.50, POCKET MAP J7
174 Johnston Rd, Wan Chai Ⓜ Wan Chai,
Exit A3. Ⓦ kichantea.com.

Polished wooden counters and tea
leaves stored in metal cylinders set
the scene in this traditional, long-
established shop.

Lane Crawford

MAP P.50, POCKET MAP F7
Shop 126, Pacific Place 2, 88 Queensway,
Wan Chai Ⓜ Admiralty, Exit C1.

Hong Kong's oldest Western-style
department store, with a well-
stocked inventory of smart – if
sometimes stuffy – designer brands
from around the globe.

Lee Gardens

MAP P.50, POCKET MAP L7
Yun Ping Rd, Causeway Bay Ⓜ Causeway
Bay, Exit F.

Two huge towers housing upmarket
shopping malls and a selection of
good restaurants.

Sogo

MAP P.50, POCKET MAP L6
555 Hennessy Rd, Causeway Bay Ⓜ
Causeway Bay, Exit D. Daily 10am–10pm.

Hong Kong's first Japanese
department store, an enormous
complex on thirteen floors which
seems to sell just about everything.

Times Square

MAP P.50, POCKET MAP K7
Russell St, Causeway Bay Ⓜ Causeway
Bay, Exit A.

Over two hundred shops on sixteen
floors, featuring all of Hong Kong's
major brands, plus plenty of
international ones as well.

Vivienne Tam

MAP P.50, POCKET MAP L6
Shop G17, Fashion Walk, 11–19 Great
George St, Causeway Bay Ⓜ Causeway Bay,
Exit A. Ⓦ viviennetam.com.

Funky shirts and dresses in
David Hockney-meets-Vivienne

place is renowned for its traditional
Cantonese mooncakes.

Westwood style, often featuring Chairman Mao and other icons of the East. Pricey.

Restaurants

Bowrington Road Market

MAP P.50, POCKET MAP K7
Bowrington Rd, Wan Chai Ⓜ Causeway Bay, Exit A. Daily 24hr.
A full-on, bustling Chinese produce market wedged in between busy roads and flyovers, with a cooked food area upstairs selling inexpensive one-dish meals and noodle soups.

Cinta-J

MAP P.50, POCKET MAP H7
G/F, Malaysia Building, 69 Jaffe Rd, Wan Chai Ⓜ Wan Chai, Exit A1 ☎ 2529 6622. Sun–Thurs 11am–3am, Fri & Sat 11am–4am.
Legendary Indonesian and Filipino restaurant-bar, with a fantastic live band after dark most nights. Mains around $70; their sweet chilli squid and sour fish soup are the genuine article.

Coyote

MAP P.500, POCKET MAP H7
114–120 Lockhart Rd, Wan Chai Ⓜ Wan Chai, Exit C ☎ 2861 2221. Daily noon–2am.
Lively Tex-Mex bar and grill with good barbecued ribs, full of margarita-quaffing patrons digging into plates of tortillas and grilled steaks.

Crystal Jade

MAP P.50, POCKET MAP L7
Basement 2, Times Square, Causeway Bay Ⓜ Causeway Bay, Exit A ☎ 2506 0080. Daily 11am–11pm.
Popular branch of a city-wide Shanghainese snack chain, serving excellent *xiaolongbao* – steamed pork dumplings in a thin, wheat-dough wrapper – and spicy noodle soups ($60).

Drunken Jade Restaurant

MAP P.50, POCKET MAP J7

289 Hennessy Rd, Causeway Bay Ⓜ Wan Chai, Exit A2 ☎ 2511 1848. Daily 7am–11pm.
Don't be put off by the lack of English signage (look for 醉瓊樓酒家); this small restaurant serves great Hakka-style *dim sum* and one-pot set meals for around $150 a head.

Fook Lam Moon

MAP P.50, POCKET MAP H7
35–45 Johnston Rd, Wan Chai Ⓜ Wan Chai, Exit B ☎ 2866 0663. Daily 11.30am–3pm & 6–11pm.
Among Hong Kong's most famous Cantonese restaurants. House specialities include bird's nest in coconut milk, abalone, crispy piglet and crisp-skinned chicken. Count on $800 a head.

Harmony Village Vegetarian

MAP P.50, POCKET MAP L7
11/F Jardine Centre, 50 Jardine's Bazaar, Causeway Bay Ⓜ Causeway Bay, Exit F. ☎ 2881 5698. Daily 11.30am–11pm.
Buddhist vegetarian place – no onions or garlic – seating just fifteen, with a lunchtime set meal featuring unlimited rice for around $55.

Hay! (喜遇)

MAP P.50, POCKET MAP H8
G01, Lee Tung Ave Ⓜ Wan Chai Exit A3 ☎ 2388 3666, ⓦ welovehay.com. Daily 11.45am–10.30pm.
Shanghai snacks – drunken chicken, four-treasures *kaofu*, egg white and broadbeans, *xiaolongbao* – served in a bright, informal, busy environment. About $100 a head.

Hee Kee

MAP P.50, POCKET MAP K6
379 Jaffe Rd, Causeway Bay Ⓜ Causeway Bay, Exit C ☎ 2893 7565. Daily noon–midnight.
Minimalist location for consuming deep-fried whole crab with chillies ($600), said to be an old Causeway Bay speciality. Sporadically popular with Hong Kong film stars.

Kung Tak Lam

MAP P.50, POCKET MAP L6

10/F, World Trade Centre, Causeway Bay
Ⓜ Causeway Bay, Exit E ☎ 2881 9966. Daily
11am–11pm.

Shanghai-style vegetarian restaurant
specializing in "meat" dishes,
though the food – while tasty
enough – is nowhere near as good
as the view out over the harbour.
Expect $150 a head.

Lei Garden

MAP P.50, POCKET MAP K7

1/F, CNT Tower, 338 Hennessy Road, Wan
Chai Ⓜ Wan Chai Exit A3. ☎ 2892 0333.
Daily 11.30am–3pm & 6–11pm.

Long-running chain with a very good
standard of Chaozhou-style *dim
sum*, including crispy-skinned pork,
cheung fan stuffed rice rolls, fried
turnip cake and transparent *fun gwor*.

Metropol

MAP P.50, POCKET MAP F7

4/F, United Centre, 95 Queensway, Wan Chai
Ⓜ Admiralty, Exit D ☎ 2865 1988. Daily
8am–midnight.

Huge *dim sum* hall, very child-
friendly, with views of Convention
Centre. Try the flaky *char siu*
pastries and crunchy prawn
dumplings, served from trollies.

The Pawn

MAP P.50, POCKET MAP H7

62 Johnston Rd, Wan Chai Ⓜ Wan Chai, Exit
A3 ☎ 2866 3444, Ⓦ thepawn.com.hk Daily
11.30am–11pm.

Smart, rather precious pub in a
restored nineteenth century Chinese
pawnbroker's. Admire the views
from the balcony, knock back a cold
Hong Kong Underground Pale Ale,
and tuck into their modern British
menu. Count on spending $500.

Plaza Mayor

MAP P.50, POCKET MAP G7

9 Moon St, Wan Chai Ⓜ Wan Chai, Exit B1 or
B2 ☎ 2866 6644, Ⓦ plazamayor.hk. Mon–
Sat 11am–midnight, Sun 6pm–midnight.

Tiny place with black-and-white
tiling, a marble counter, excellent
tapas – try the *iberico* ham and
garlic shrimps – and good Spanish
wine. $250 a head.

Shuangxi Lou (雙喜樓)

MAP P.50, POCKET MAP H7

Shop G32, Lee Tung Ave Ⓜ Wan Chai Exit
A3 ☎ 2805 8828. Daily 11.30am–11pm.

Bright, modern restaurant serving
traditional Cantonese *dim sum* – go
for the steamed spare ribs, crispy-
skinned pork and meltingly soft
char siu pork. $120 per head.

Wing Wah (永華麵家)

MAP P.50, POCKET MAP B6

89 Hennessy Rd, Wan Chai Ⓜ Wan Chai, Exit
B ☎ 2527 7476. Mon–Sat noon–2am.

Locally famous for its wonton
noodle soup ($34), which is what
they'll bring you by default unless
you ask for something else – such as
their sweet red bean and tangerine
peel soup.

Bars and clubs

Café Gray Deluxe

MAP P.50, POCKET MAP F7

Level 49, Pacific Place, 88 Queensway, Wan
Chai Ⓜ Admiralty, Exit C1 ☎ 3968 1106.
Daily 6.30am–10.30pm.

The bar of this romantic restaurant
is proof that the area has a greater
choice of places to drink than its
"sweaty dive" reputation suggests.
Choose from their range of classic
wines and cocktails, enjoy a bar
snack and look out over the city.

Carnegie's

MAP P.50, POCKET MAP H7

53–55 Lockhart Rd, Wan Chai Ⓜ Wan Chai,
Exit C ☎ 2866 6289. Mon–Thurs 11am–
late, Sat noon–late, Sun 5pm–late.

The noise level here means
conversation is only possible via
flash cards; once it's packed, hordes
of punters keen to revel the night
away fight for dancing space on the
bar. Hosts the occasional riotous
club night and regular live music.

Devil's Advocate

MAP P.50, POCKET MAP H7

48–50 Lockhart Rd, Wan Chai Ⓜ Wan Chai, Exit C ☎ 2865 7271. Daily noon–1am.
Long-running, raucously popular sports' bar which attracts a younger crowd. If you can cope with the terrible 1970s soundtrack, come along during the happy hour (daily noon–9pm) for excellent deals or on Wednesdays for further discounts.

Dickens Sports Bar

MAP P.50, POCKET MAP L6
Lower Ground Floor, Excelsior Hotel, 281 Gloucester Rd, Causeway Bay Ⓜ Causeway Bay, Exit D1 ☎ 2837 6782. Mon–Thurs & Sun 11am–2am, Fri & Sat 11am–3am.
This bar prides itself on re-creating an authentic British atmosphere: the kitchen dishes up genuine British pub grub (such as Cumberland sausages, mash and gravy), the TV airs British sitcoms, and there are English papers to read.

Dusk Till Dawn

MAP P.50, POCKET MAP H7
76 Jaffe Rd, Wan Chai Ⓜ Wan Chai, Exit C ☎ 2528 4689. Mon–Sat noon–6am, Sun 3pm–6am; happy hour 5–11pm.
Vaguely Mediterranean colours decorate this rowdy bar, full of loud live music, raucous staff and hoarse punters.

Joe Banana's

MAP P.50, POCKET MAP H7
23 Luard Rd Ⓜ Wan Chai, Exit C ☎ 2529 1811. Mon–Fri noon–5am, Sat & Sun 5pm–5am.
British-style bar with a late disco, fake palms and regular live music. You need to be (or look) 21 to get in and there's a strict door policy – men need a shirt with a collar.

TED's Lookout

MAP P.50, POCKET MAP G7
G/F, Moonful Court, 17A Moon St, Wan Chai Ⓜ Wan Chai, Exit B2 ☎ 2520 0076. Daily 8am–11pm.
Cute – or just plain small – restaurant-bar in a quiet cul-de-sac; the Tex-Mex style food is above average, but the drinks are superb, if pricey.

Wanch

MAP P.50, POCKET MAP G7
54 Jaffe Rd Ⓜ Wan Chai, Exit C ☎ 2861 1621, Ⓦ thewanch.hk. Mon–Sat 11am–2am, Sun noon–2am.
A Wan Chai institution, this tiny, unpretentious bar is jostling and friendly and has live music – usually folk and rock – every night. Also serves cheap, chunky cheeseburgers and sandwiches ($30).

Carnegie's

Hong Kong Island: the south side

Hong Kong Island's south side, while not undeveloped, still offers an escape from the north shore's densely packed high-rises. Aberdeen has a long maritime tradition, and the coastal stretch between here and the tourist enclave of Stanley is punctured by sandy bays and inlets, though you'll have to share them with crowds at the weekend. The beaches are pretty enough, however, and there's further distraction in one of Hong Kong's two theme parks – a great place to spend a day if you have kids in tow. The island's southeast corner has managed to remain as rural as anything can be on Hong Kong Island, featuring a bracing ridgetop hike, some almost wild coastal scenery and a superb beach out around Shek O.

Aberdeen

MAP P.60
Bus #7 from Outer Islands Ferry Pier, Central; #70 from Exchange Square, Central; or #72 from Moreton Terrace, Causeway Bay.

Aberdeen was already settled when the British arrived in the 1840s – the bay here was used by

Aberdeen

the indigenous Hoklos and Tankas, who fished in the surrounding archipelago. The harbour remains Aberdeen's focus, surrounded by a forest of tall apartment blocks and full of freshly cleaned fishing vessels during the July fishing moratorium – which is also when you can catch the annual **Dragon Boat Festival**.

Aberdeen's harbourside **fish market** (busiest before 10am) is an incredible sight, where trawlers disgorge their catches and have them sorted into rows of buckets, tanks and trays, among which wholesale buyers poke and prod. Some of the catch is recognisable, some downright unbelievable – bring a camera and, if you have them, waterproof shoes.

Along the waterfront you'll be approached by women selling **sampan rides** (about $60 per person after bargaining). These cruise the straits between Aberdeen and **Ap Lei Chau island** (Ⓜ Ap Lei Chau) opposite – full of discount clothing warehouses – offering views of

Ocean Park

trawlers complete with dogs, drying laundry and outdoor kitchens. You can get a similar trip for free by catching the ferry from beside the fish market to one of Aberdeen's **floating restaurants**, moored around the side of Ap Lei Chau. The ostentatious *Jumbo Floating Restaurant* is the best-known (see page 63).

Ocean Park

MAP P.60
Bus #629 from Central Ferry Piers
oceanpark.com.hk. Daily 10am–6pm.
$438, under-11s $219; includes all rides and entry.

Filling a whole peninsula, **Ocean Park** is an open-air theme park and oceanarium; it also features four **giant pandas**, for whom a special two-thousand-square-metre complex has been created.

The park is split into themed zones – Aqua City, Amazing Asian Animals, Rainforest, Marine World etc. You enter into the **Lowland**, which is where to catch Chinese wildlife – including the pandas, bizarre golden monkeys,

and Yangtze alligators – plus investigate an aviary and the first of several aquariums. From here, a cablecar hoists you 1.5km up the mountainside to the Summit and its scary Dragon rollercoaster and the self-explanatory "Abyss Turbo Drop". Overlooking the headland is one of the world's largest reef aquariums, currently featuring a variety of giant rays and sharks – not to mention tanks of Chinese sturgeon fish, rescued from the brink of extinction by farming. The rest of the park (linked by one of the longest outdoor escalators in the world) gives access to Polar Adventure, featuring arctic foxes, and a variety of funfair rides; the Raging River Ride will leave you absolutely soaked.

Repulse Bay

MAP P.60
Bus #6, #6A, #61, #64 or #260 from Exchange Square, Central.

Increasingly built up with tower blocks, **Repulse Bay** is named after the British warship HMS

Stanley market

Repulse, which mopped up local pirates in the nineteenth century and later the area was known for the cocktail parties held at the grand *Repulse Bay Hotel*. The hotel has since been demolished and **The Repulse Bay** erected on its remains, a wavy apartment block with a square hole through the centre, designed along *feng shui* principles (see page 34).

The beach is clean and wide, though on summer afternoons hordes of people descend on the sands. Connoisseurs of kitsch may want to amble down to the little Chinese garden at the end of the prom, where a brightly painted group of goddesses, Buddha statues, stone lions and dragons offer some tempting photo opportunities. If the crowds are too much, try the nearby beaches at **Middle Bay** and **South Bay**, fifteen minutes' and thirty minutes' walk south around the bay respectively.

Stanley

MAP P.60
Bus #6, #6A or #260 from Exchange

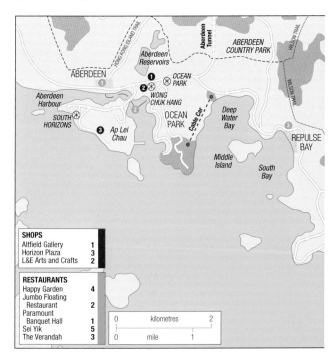

SHOPS

Altfield Gallery	1
Horizon Plaza	3
L&E Arts and Crafts	2

RESTAURANTS

Happy Garden	4
Jumbo Floating Restaurant	2
Paramount Banquet Hall	1
Sei Yik	5
The Verandah	3

Square, Central.

When Britain seized Hong Kong there were already two thousand people living at the south coast settlement of **Stanley**, earning an income from fishing and piracy. Today, it's a small residential place, with low-key modern buildings surrounding Stanley Plaza and **Murray House**, built in 1843 for the British Army and relocated stone by stone in 1982 from its previous site in Central, where the Bank of China now stands.

To the east, Stanley's touristy **market** (daily 10am–7pm) straddles the streets and alleys around Stanley Market Street, and is a good place to pick up clothing, bright tack and souvenirs. Often overlooked, the small **Tin Hau Temple** on the western side of the plaza dates from 1767. Typically, Tin Hau's statue has to share the hall with a dozen other deities of Taoist,

Buddhist and local origins, along with a darkened tiger pelt, bagged nearby in 1942 – the last ever shot in Hong Kong. There are also lanterns and model ships, reminding you of Tin Hau's role as protector of fishermen, though there's little fishing done from Stanley these days. Stanley's best stretch of sand is **St Stephen's Beach**, fifteen minutes south along the shore, with a short pier, watersports centre, barbecue pits, showers and decent swimming. On the headland above, **Stanley Prison** was notorious during World War II, when hundreds of civilians were interned here in dire conditions by the Japanese.

The Dragon's Back

MAP P.60
Bus #9 from Shau Kei Wan (next to the MTR station) or Shek O.

The Dragon's Back is the final section of the 50km-long **Hong**

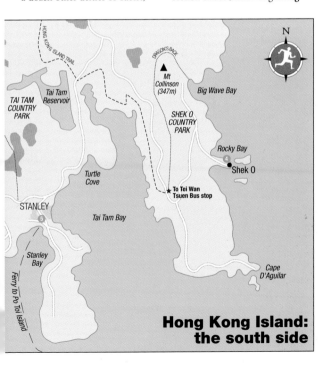

Hong Kong Island: the south side

Kong Island Trail, which runs west to east across the island. Though the name sounds fierce, the two-hour hike is not too difficult, and at weekends you're likely to find plenty of other people tackling it. Conditions are exposed and can be hot, however, so take water and a hat.

Get off the bus at the **To Tei Wan Tsuen** stop, where there's a roadside parking bay and a map of the route, then follow the track up through woodland and scrub out onto the Dragon's Back itself.

This ridge runs north past granite outcrops, taking in views of Stanley town, green hills and fantastic seascapes, before skirting the rear of Mount Collison and descending to **Big Wave Bay**'s beaches. From here, it's a half-hour stroll south to Shek O.

Shek O

MAP P.60
Bus #9 from Shau Kei Wan (next to the MTR station); or Sun only bus #309

from Exchange Square, Central (hourly 2.10–6.10pm; last bus back departs Shek O at 7pm).

Shek O is an unpretentious village down at Hong Kong's southeastern reaches, with the best beach on the island. Wide, with white sand and fringed by shady trees, it can get very full at the weekend. There are also a few restaurants and expat bars in the village, and on Sunday extra snack stalls open, serving the crowds who come down to swim. Unsurprisingly, Shek O is one of the most desirable addresses in Hong Kong, and there are some upmarket pieces of real estate in the area. You can get a flavour of things by walking through the village parallel with the beach and following the path up to **Shek O Headland** for some sweeping panoramas.

For more space and fewer people, **Big Wave Bay** is a half-hour walk north of Shek O, with another good beach, barbecue pits and a refreshment kiosk.

Shek O Headland

Shops

Altfield Gallery

MAP P.60

9th Floor, Gee Chang Hong Centre, 65 Wong Chuk Hang Rd, Aberdeen. Call first ☎ 2552 1968, ⓦ altfield.com.hk.

Quality antiques from a dealer specializing in China and Southeast Asia. Everything from statues and maps to jewellery, but none of it a bargain.

Horizon Plaza

MAP P.60

2 Lee Wing St, Ap Lei Chau island. Ⓜ South Horizons, Exit C ☎ 2554 9089, ⓦ horizonplazahk.com. Daily 10am–7pm.

25 storeys of discount furnishings and designer fashion labels – Hong Kong's major upmarket clothing stores, such as *Joyce Boutique* (21/F), send all last season's stock here. Also try the *Old Shanghai* (15/F) and *Oriental Chest* (12/F).

L&E Arts and Crafts

MAP P.60

11A Kwai Bo Industrial Building, 40 Wong Chuk Hang Rd, Aberdeen, Call first ☎ 2546 9886, ⓦ lneco.com

Stalwart of antique – and antique-style – home furnishings; a great place for a browse.

Restaurants

Happy Garden

MAP P.60

Near the bus stop, Shek O ☎ 2809 4165. Daily noon–10pm.

One of several laidback places with outdoor tables, luridly coloured drinks and excellent food – try the water spinach with *belechan* beef, or huge Thai fish cakes. Mains cost around $100.

Jumbo Floating Restaurant

MAP P.60

Shum Wan Pier Drive, Wong Chuk Hang. Bus #75 from Exchange Square, Central, to Shum Wan Pier, then take an on-demand ferry; restaurant pays the homeward taxi fare if you spend enough on your meal. ☎ 2553 9111, ⓦ jumbokingdom.com. Mon–Sat 11am–11.30pm, Sun 9am–11.30pm.

A Hong Kong institution, this ridiculously ostentatious mess of golden dragons, florid rooflines and auspicious red decor is best seen at night, lit up like a Christmas tree. Their Cantonese food is competent rather than memorable, but set menus are not too expensive (around $600 a head) and it's fun as a one-off experience. Alternatively, the *dim sum* menu will only set you back around $30 a plate.

Paramount Banquet Hall

MAP P.60

Shop F, 1/F, Phase 5, Aberdeen Centre, Hoi Lung Court, Nam Ning St. ☎ 2884 9088. Daily 6am–midnight.

Huge, bright, noisy mid-range place to wolf down an excellent *dim sum* breakfast; just watch out for the over-active a/c. Above average seafood and roast meats.

Sei Yik (泗益)

MAP P.60

Stanley Market, Stanley ☎ 2813 0507. Daily 6am–4pm.

There's no English sign for this legendary hole-in-the-wall, which serves Hong Kong style French toast, milk tea and beef-and-egg sandwiches – just a few local snacks that are rarely served up elsewhere these days.

The Verandah

MAP P.60

109 Repulse Bay Rd, Repulse Bay ☎ 2292 2822. Wed–Sat noon–10.pm, Sun 11am–10pm.

Famous for its lavish Sunday brunches, afternoon teas and candle-lit dinners, this elegant establishment features colonial ambience in the dark wooden furniture, shutters and long sea views from the shaded balcony. Don't miss their Grand Marnier soufflé or the oysters.

Kowloon: Tsim Sha Tsui

Kowloon, from the Cantonese *gau lung* ("nine dragons", after an undulating ridge of hills here), was a twelve-square-kilometre peninsula on the Chinese mainland north of Hong Kong Island when the British seized it in 1860. Land reclamation has since more than doubled its size and Kowloon has become the most densely populated place on earth, nowhere more obvious than in the frenetic waterfront district of Tsim Sha Tsui, where many visitors stay, eat and – especially – shop. The quantity and variety of goods on sale here is staggering, and a devoted window-shopper can find every bauble, electronic gadget and designer label known to man. If it all sounds too gruesomely commercial, there's solace in the Cultural Centre and several museums, while Tsim Sha Tsui's waterfront provides one of the best views of Central's skyline.

Star Ferry Pier and Canton Road

MAP P.66, POCKET MAP A18
Ⓜ Tsim Sha Tsui, Exit J6.
Tsim Sha Tsui's **Star Ferry Pier** is sited at Kowloon's south-western tip; immediately outside is a 45m-high clocktower, dating from 1921, the only remnant of the grand train station which

Afternoon tea in the Peninsula Hong Kong

once welcomed European rail services. The ferry terminal sits at the bottom of a series of interconnected, upmarket shopping malls, known as **Canton Road**, running up the western side of Tsim Sha Tsui's waterfront. The first section, **Ocean Terminal**, is where cruise liners dock, while the next two blocks up – **Ocean Centre** and **Harbour City** – between them form a maze of galleries, hotels, restaurants and pricey boutiques. At the far end, the **China Ferry Terminal** comprises another block of stores where ferries depart for China and Macau.

The Peninsula Hotel

MAP P.66, POCKET MAP B18
Salisbury Rd Ⓜ Tsim Sha Tsui, Exit J6
☎ 2920 2888, Ⓦ peninsula.com.
Harking back to colonial times, **The Peninsula Hotel** was built in the 1920s beside the old train station, offering a shot of elegance to Hong Kong's weary new arrivals who had spent weeks crossing Europe, Russia and China. It

Architecture at the Hong Kong Cultural Centre

remains one of the most stylish addresses in Hong Kong, and serves **afternoon tea** in the opulent Baroque lobby (daily 2–6pm, $368 per person) – note that dress rules apply (see page 65).

The Hong Kong Cultural Centre

MAP P.66, POCKET MAP A18

Salisbury Rd Ⓜ Tsim Sha Tsui, Exit J4
☎ 2734 2009, Ⓦ hkculturalcentre.gov.hk.
Box office daily 9am–9pm.

The Hong Kong Cultural Centre was built in 1980 to provide a cultural hub for this otherwise overtly materialistic city. It contains a concert hall and several theatres, where events from classical Italian and Chinese opera through to contemporary dance are performed (contact the box office for current programmes). Worthy though all this is, the building itself proves that you need vision to create impressive architecture: astonishingly, given the dramatic harbourside location, the building has no windows. The pink-tiled exterior is awkwardly shaped, with angled walls and outshooting ribs creating a cloister surrounded by a starkly paved area, dotted with palm trees. An adjacent two-tiered

Afternoon tea

Heading to a smart hotel for British-style afternoon tea is a Hong Kong institution. The *Peninsula* is the most magnificent and "traditional" option, but there's also the *InterContinental* (Salisbury Rd, Tsim Sha Tsui); the *Island Shangri-La* (Two Pacific Place, 88 Queensway, Central); the *Tiffin Lounge* at the *Grand Hyatt* (Harbour Rd, Wan Chai); and the *Mandarin Oriental* (Connaught Rd, Central). You'll pay upwards of $350 per person. **Dress code** is "smart casual", ruling out shorts, sportswear, sandals, flip-flops and blue jeans.

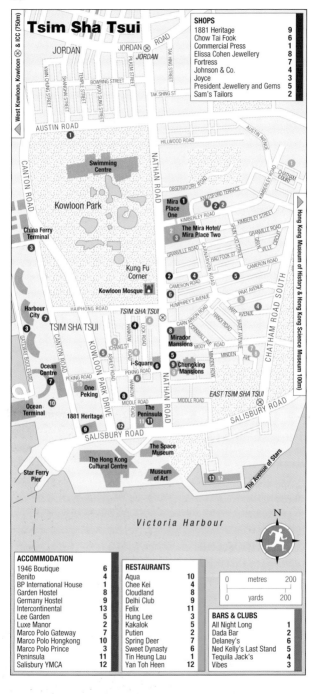

Tsim Sha Tsui

SHOPS

1881 Heritage	9
Chow Tai Fook	6
Commercial Press	1
Elissa Cohen Jewellery	8
Fortress	7
Johnson & Co.	4
Joyce	3
President Jewellery and Gems	5
Sam's Tailors	2

West Kowloon, Kowloon ⊗ & ICC (750m)

Hong Kong Museum of History & Hong Kong Science Museum 100m)

Victoria Harbour

ACCOMMODATION

1946 Boutique	6
Benito	4
BP International House	1
Garden Hostel	8
Germany Hostel	9
Intercontinental	13
Lee Garden	5
Luxe Manor	2
Marco Polo Gateway	7
Marco Polo Hongkong	10
Marco Polo Prince	3
Peninsula	11
Salisbury YMCA	12

RESTAURANTS

Aqua	10
Chee Kei	4
Cloudland	8
Delhi Club	9
Felix	11
Hung Lee	3
Kakalok	5
Putien	2
Spring Deer	7
Sweet Dynasty	6
Tin Heung Lau	1
Yan Toh Heen	12

0	metres	200
0	yards	200

BARS & CLUBS

All Night Long	1
Dada Bar	2
Delaney's	6
Ned Kelly's Last Stand	5
Tequila Jack's	4
Vibes	3

N

walkway along the water offers the view of the harbour and Hong Kong Island denied from the inside; come here at night to see Central's towers in all their chromatic glory.

Museum of Art

MAP P.66, POCKET MAP B18
10 Salisbury Rd Ⓜ Tsim Sha Tsui, Exit J4 Ⓦ lcsd.gov.hk. Closed for renovation until mid-2019; check website for temporary exhibitions from the collection.

Hong Kong's **Museum of Art** houses six galleries of mostly classical Chinese works, with frequent touring exhibitions, often featuring masterpieces from collections on the mainland and Taiwan.

The first-floor **Chinese Antiquities Gallery** has an ever-changing exhibition of gold, jade and bronzes, many dating back several thousand years to the semi-mythical Shang, Xia and Zhou dynasties. The second floor's **Xubaizhai Gallery** concentrates on silk scroll painting and calligraphy; it's the spirit of the brush-strokes, rather than the subject itself, which is most admired. The adjacent **Contemporary Art Gallery** features post-1950s work, but in so many styles and going in so many directions that it's hard to tell what is important and what is just whimsy.

There's another staid but informative **Antiquities Gallery** on the third floor, strong on pottery: Neolithic clay pots with black patterns; lively Han figurines and tomb models of houses and watchtowers; and designs that, artistically at least, peaked with the Tang's abstract colours and the Song's simplicity. Also on the third floor, the **Historical Pictures Gallery** has a rotating selection of paintings, drawings and prints that trace the eighteenth- and nineteenth-century development of Hong Kong, Macau and Guangzhou as trading centres, as seen by both Western and local artists. The museum ends on the

Exhibits at the Hong Kong Museum of Art

fourth floor with the **Chinese Fine Art Gallery**, which shows exhibits from a collection of three thousand works, including modern Chinese art, and animal and bird paintings.

Space Museum

MAP P.66, POCKET MAP B18
Salisbury Rd Ⓜ Tsim Sha Tsui, Exit J4.
☎ 2721 0226, Ⓦ lcsd.gov.hk. Closed until late 2018 for renovation; check website for details.

The Chinese were the first to record Halley's Comet and the first to chart star movements – the **Space Museum** traces these breakthroughs and the entire history of astronomy with hands-on displays, push-button exhibits, video presentations and picture boards. There's also a **Space Theatre**, where an ever-changing selection of films (either on space or the natural world) is shown on the massive wraparound Omnimax screen, providing a thrilling sensory experience.

The Avenue of Stars

MAP P.66, POCKET MAP C18
Salisbury Rd Ⓜ Tsim Sha Tsui, Exit J4.
Hong Kong's film industry was once the third-largest in the world, and this waterfront promenade celebrates its heroes with pavement handprints and brass name plaques to luminaries such as Jackie Chan, Chow Yun Fat, Maggie Cheung, Wong Kar Wai and Raymond Chow. The biggest draw, however, is the **statue of Bruce Lee**, who catapulted the industry – and Chinese kung fu – to world attention in the 1970s; watch young Chinese striking a pose alongside for photos. The Avenue is also a great place to catch the nightly **Symphony of Lights** (8pm; free), when Central's coloured skyscrapers pulse and flash to a synthesized beat.

Nathan Road

MAP P.66, POCKET MAP B14–B18
Ⓜ Tsim Sha Tsui.

Nathan Road

Old children's toys on display at the Hong Kong Museum of History

Nathan Road is Tsim Sha Tsui's – and Kowloon's – main thoroughfare, running north for 3km from the waterfront to Boundary Street. The pavements are always packed with extraordinarily thick crowds and the roads with fast-moving traffic. It's not just the neon along here that glitters, but the shop windows too, full of jewellery, the latest cameras and mobile phones, clothes, shoes and fine art. Even window-shopping is a struggle nonetheless, what with the crowds, hustlers and the insistent hawkers.

Nathan Road has its own **shopping centres**, the most notorious of which are the seething downmarket complexes of Chungking Mansions (nos. 36–44) and Mirador Mansions (nos. 56–58), full of guesthouses, Indian restaurants and super-cheap stalls for daily necessities. Side streets are also alive with similar possibilities. To the east of Nathan Road, **Granville Road** is famous for its bargain clothes shops, some of them showcasing the work of new, young designers, though you'll also find clothing, accessory and jewellery stores all the way along Carnarvon, Cameron and Kimberley roads.

Hong Kong Museum of History

MAP P.66, POCKET MAP C16
Chatham Rd South Ⓜ Tsim Sha Tsui,
Exit B2/Hung Hom, Exit D6 Ⓦ hk.history.
museum. Mon & Wed–Fri 10am–6pm, Sat
& Sun 10am–7pm. Free, except special
exhibitions

The **Hong Kong Museum of History** is an ambitious trawl through the region's past, using videos, light shows, interactive software and life-sized reconstructions. Things kick off with rainforest, which covered the island millions of years ago, then human development from the Stone Age, via early contact with mainland China during the Han dynasty, through to scale models of wooden junks that filled Hong Kong harbour until recent times, and a reproduction of a 1930s street complete with tea shops that smell of tea. Perhaps what's most striking is that these shops don't look much different from those in business in Mong Kok and Sheung

China's martial arts

China's many **martial arts** mostly trace their origins back to Henan province's Shaolin Temple, where, according to legend, the sixth-century monk Bodhidharma developed exercises to balance the inactivity of meditation. These evolved into fighting routines for defending the temple, and were gradually disseminated into the rest of China.

Early morning is the best time to catch people training – Kowloon and Victoria parks are especially popular. The large groups moving slowly through their routines are doing tai chi; specifically local styles include *wing chun* – which became famous as being the first martial art Bruce Lee studied – and *hung gar*, associated with the nineteenth-century master Wong Fei Hung.

Wan today, almost a hundred years later.

Hong Kong Science Museum

MAP P.66, POCKET MAP C16
Chatham Rd South Ⓜ Tsim Sha Tsui, Exit B2/Hung Hom, Exit D6 Ⓦ hk.science. museum. Mon & Wed–Fri 10am–7pm, Sat & Sun 10am–9pm. $20, Wed free.

With four floors full of things to prod, pull and take to pieces, the **Hong Kong Science Museum** is really somewhere to bring children for a couple of hours – especially if it's raining. Each level has themed exhibitions exploring electricity, optical illusions, engineering (a very Hong Kong topic) and the like, in fun, hands-on ways. The seemingly easy 3D puzzles will keep even the adults busy for a while, while the Energy Machine features wooden balls racing around the entire museum along a giant maze of tracks, buckets, pulleys, drums and gongs – ask at the desk for performance times.

Kowloon Park

MAP P.66, POCKET MAP A16–B17
Ⓜ Tsim Sha Tsui, Exit A1. Daily 5am–midnight.

Kung Fu in Kowloon Park

Find an escape from the teeming masses in **Kowloon Park**, which stretches along Nathan Road between Haiphong and Austin roads. Parts of it have been landscaped and styled as a Chinese garden with fountains, rest areas, a children's playground, and two bird collections – the wildfowl (including flamingos and mandarin ducks) outside in landscaped ponds, the parrots and other exotically coloured rainforest species contained in a small aviary. There's also a swimming complex (daily 6.30am–noon, 1–5pm & 6–10pm; $19) and a sculpture walk.

The southeastern corner of the park is taken up with an open area known as the **Kung Fu Corner**. Full of practitioners from about 6am every morning, it also hosts free displays of various martial arts between 2.30pm and 4.30pm every Sunday. Below it, at 105 Nathan Road, is the large **Kowloon Mosque** (no public access), built in the mid-1980s to replace a mosque originally built in 1894 for the British Army's Muslim troops from India.

West Kowloon

MAP P.66, POCKET MAP A16
Ⓜ Kowloon

Awkward to reach from Tsim Sha Tsui, though centred around the Kowloon MTR station, **West Kowloon** is an area of half-finished parkland and paving, slated as the future site of (amongst other things) the Beijing-funded **Imperial**

View from Sky100, ICC

Palace Museum. It's already unmissable, thanks to the silver, towering **ICC** – the International Commerce Centre – Hong Kong's tallest building at 484m. A lift from the Elements Mall below whisks you 393m up to the **Sky100 viewing deck** (Ⓦ sky100.com.hk; Sun–Thurs 10am–9pm, Fri & Sat 10am–10.30pm; $168) in just a few seconds, providing truly stunning views of the outer islands, Kowloon, the whole north shore of Hong Kong (and, of course, the shorter IFC2 tower opposite), ferries and harbour traffic. Sunset is always a good time, or any day with patchy cloud – which brings alive the seascapes to the west.

Tailors and suits

As you'll realize after being harassed by touts every few paces along Nathan Road, Tsim Sha Tsui hosts an abundance of tailors specializing in making suits for visitors. Many produce excellent work, but bear a few things in mind: suits made in 24 hours tend to fall apart just as quickly (three days is a realistic minimum, and should involve a couple of fittings); prices for good work are good value but not cheap (expect to pay about the same as an off-the-peg suit at home); and you'll usually have to pay half the cost up front as a deposit.

Shops

1881 Heritage

MAP P.66, POCKET MAP A18
East of Canton Rd, between Salisbury & Peking roads Ⓜ Tsim Sha Tsui, Exit I3.
Outdoor shopping mall based around the site of the former Marine Police Station (whose reconstruction is the centrepiece), brimming with upmarket boutiques.

Chow Tai Fook

MAP P.66, POCKET MAP B17
i-Square, 63 Nathan Rd Ⓜ Tsim Sha Tsui, Exit D1. Ⓦ chowtaifook.com/en
Chain with a wide range of gold, diamond and jade jewellery at mid-range prices – a good place to get a feel for local styles and costs.

Commercial Press

MAP P.66, POCKET MAP B17
Basement, Mira Place One, 132–134 Nathan Rd Ⓜ Tsim Sha Tsui, Exit B1. Daily 11am–9pm.
Bright, modern bookshop with a broad range of photo-heavy coffee-table works and local literature in English, plus a great selection of Chinese-language titles.

Elissa Cohen Jewellery

MAP P.66, POCKET MAP B18
209 Hankow Centre, 5–15 Hankow Rd Ⓜ Tsim Sha Tsui, Exit L3. Ⓦ elissacohen.com
Individual and very elegant designs, either new or based on antique European or Chinese styles.

Fortress

MAP P.66, POCKET MAP A17
Level 3, Ocean Centre, Canton Rd Ⓜ Tsim Sha Tsui, Exit L3. Ⓦ fortress.com.hk
A local electronics chain selling the latest mobiles, MP3 players, digital cameras and laptops. No bargains, but you won't get ripped off either; a good indicator of what to pay locally.

Johnson & Co.

MAP P.66, POCKET MAP B17
44 Hankow Rd Ⓜ Tsim Sha Tsui, Exit A1.
Tailoring for mostly male customers (they were a favourite with British military personnel stationed in Hong Kong), this shop also deals

1881 Heritage

in middle-of-the-road jewellery and watches.

Joyce

MAP P.66, POCKET MAP A17
G106 Gateway Arcade, Harbour City, Canton Rd Ⓜ Tsim Sha Tsui, Exit C1. Ⓦ Joyce.com
Hong Kong's most fashionable boutique offers its own range of clothing, as well as many top overseas designer brands.

President Jewellery and Gems

MAP P.66, POCKET MAP B17
Shop G16, Holiday Inn Golden Mile Mall, 50 Nathan Rd Ⓜ Tsim Sha Tsui, Exit D1. Ⓣ 2366 7085.
A small, family-run business specializing in pearls and diamonds, that also gives good advice on buying high-quality jewellery in Hong Kong without getting ripped off.

Sam's Tailors

MAP P.66, POCKET MAP B17
Burlington Arcade, 90–94 Nathan Rd Ⓜ Tsim Sha Tsui, Exit B1. Ⓦ samstailor.com
A Hong Kong institution, as much for Sam's talent for self-publicity as for the quality of his clothes – he's reputed to have made suits for Bill Clinton, Jude Law and Pierce Brosnan.

Restaurants

Aqua

MAP P.66, POCKET MAP A18
29/F Penthouse, One Peking Rd MTsim Sha Tsui, Exit E Ⓣ 3427 2288, Ⓦ aqua.com.hk
Daily noon–2.30pm & 6–11pm.
Enjoy superlative harbour views from the sunken slate tables as you consume a blend of Italian and Japanese dishes. The atmosphere is informal, and the prices high – around $500 for a main.

Chee Kei

MAP P.66, POCKET MAP A17
37 Lock Rd Ⓜ Tsim Sha Tsui, Exit A1 Ⓣ 2368 2528. Daily 11am–11pm.

Aqua

Bright Chinese diner serving unpretentious, good-quality wonton and noodle soups ($60), fried pork steak, crispy prawn rolls and fishballs.

Cloudland

MAP P.66, POCKET MAP C17
Wah Fung Building, 17–23 Minden Ave Ⓜ Tsim Sha Tsui, Exit D2 Ⓣ 2722 0156.
Daily 11am–11pm.
One of Kowloon's most crowded *dim sum* places, with some unusual dishes (caterpillar fungus beef rolls) among a run of tasty stalwarts: crispy pork, seafood *congee*, prawn dumplings and even fried rice. Nice presentation too; around $200 a head.

Delhi Club

MAP P.66, POCKET MAP A17
Block C, 3/F, Chungking Mansions, 38–44 Nathan Rd Ⓜ Tsim Sha Tsui, Exit E Ⓣ 2368 1682. Daily noon–3.30pm & 6–11.30pm.
A Nepali curry house with spartan surroundings, slap-down service, and an inexpensive set meal that would feed an army. Also recommended for their vegetarian dishes, mutton and

tandoori specialties, and clay-oven-cooked naan.

Felix

MAP P.66, POCKET MAP B18
28/F, Peninsula Hotel, Salisbury Rd Ⓜ Tsim Sha Tsui, Exit E ☎ 2696 6778. Restaurant daily 6–10.30pm; bar daily 5pm–1.30am. Dress code.
Architect-designed restaurant with incredible views of Hong Kong Island which alone warrant a visit. The menu is not as good as it should be at around $800 a head, but many people just come for a Martini at the bar.

Hung Lee (洪利小廚)

MAP P.66, POCKET MAP B17
3 Pratt Avenue Ⓜ Tsim Sha Tsui Exit A2 or D2 ☎ 3956 9197. Daily 7am–2am.
One of dwindling number of *cha chaan tengs*, inexpensive restaurants serving tasty, filling meals – such as a plate of rice, barbeque pork and greens – for $60 or less.

Kakalok

MAP P.66, POCKET MAP A17
Corner of Ashley Rd and Ichang St Ⓜ Tsim Sha Tsui, Exit A. ☎ 2376 1198.

Kakalok

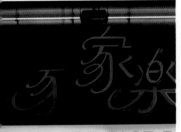

Legendary hole-in-the-wall fast-food counter which serves the cheapest fish and chips in Hong Kong ($40) – their fried noodles aren't bad either. No seats, but Kowloon Park is 100m north.

Putien (莆田)

MAP P.66, POCKET MAP B16
Shop 269–270, 2/F, Mira Place Two, 118–130 Nathan Rd Ⓜ Tsim Sha Tsui Exit B1 or B2 ☎ 3621 0825 ⓦ putien.com. Daily 11.30am–4.15pm & 5.30–10.30pm.
Expect to have to wait at this Michelin-starred *dim sum* chain, highly rated for its seasonal seafood (clam, cockles, abalone), but worth a visit at any time of year for its exquisitely presented dishes. Under $200 a head.

Spring Deer

MAP P.66, POCKET MAP C17
1/F, 42 Mody Rd Ⓜ Tsim Sha Tsui, Exit D1 ☎ 2366 4012. Daily 11.30am–3pm & 6–11pm.
Good-value place noted for its lack of decor, moderate prices and barrage of northern-Chinese favourites, such as Peking duck, baked fish on a hot plate, smoked chicken, and sugar-coated lotus seeds. Around $250 per person.

Sweet Dynasty

MAP P.66, POCKET MAP B17
Pacific Centre, 28 Hankow Rd Ⓜ Tsim Sha Tsui, Exit F ☎ 2199 7799. Mon–Fri 8am–midnight, Sat & Sun 7.30am–midnight.
Casual but smart *dim sum* restaurant specializing in Southeast Asian desserts – lots of sticky rice, coconut milk, mango puddings and sago. A bit expensive, but fun.

Tin Heung Lau (天香楼)

MAP P.66, POCKET MAP C16
18C Austin Avenue Ⓜ Jordan, Exit D ☎ 2366 2414. Daily noon–2.30pm & 6–10pm.
Not signed in English – look for the gold writing over the doorway. Unpretentious but expensive Hangzhou restaurant, whose signature dish is beggars' chicken ($400 a head; order in advance),

baked in a clay casing which is
smashed open at the table.

Yan Toh Heen

MAP P.66, POCKET MAP B18
Intercontinental Hotel, 18 Salisbury Rd
Ⓜ East Tsim Sha Tsui, Exit J2 ☎ 2313 2323.
Mon–Sat noon–2.30pm & 6–11pm, Sun
11.30am–3pm & 6–11pm.
Regarded as one of Hong Kong's
best for cutting-edge Cantonese
cooking – and for the excellent
service and harbour views. Count
on $250 a head for *dim sum*, or
$1688 for the set menu.

Bars and clubs

All Night Long

MAP P.66, POCKET MAP B16
9 Knutsford Terrace Ⓜ Tsim Sha Tsui, Exit
B1. ☎ 2367 9487. Daily 5pm–4am.
Local version of Lan Kwai Fong's
Insomnia bar, with DJs and no
fewer than eight in-house bands
playing a mix of cheesy, jazzy and
contemporary sounds to a lively
yuppie audience.

Dada Bar

MAP P.66, POCKET MAP B16
2/F Luxe Manor, 39 Kimberley Rd Ⓜ
Tsim Sha Tsui Exit B1 ☎ 3763 8778 Ⓦ
dadalounge.com.hk. Sun–Thurs 4pm–1am,
Fri & Sat 4pm–2am.
Rather fabulous lounge, with
plush velvet furniture and slightly
mad, ornate bar picked out in gold
and black. A decent wine cellar
and colourful range of cocktails
(including an "absinthe fountain"),
plus cool live music Fri & Sat after
10pm.

Delaney's

MAP P.66, POCKET MAP B17
71–77 Peking Rd Ⓜ Tsim Sha Tsui, Exit E.
Daily 8am–2am.
Large basement bar with the usual
decor, Irish beer and pub food, that
somehow manages to be more fun
than most. Good for a reasonably
quiet drink early on, though heats
up through the night.

Ned Kelly's Last Stand

Ned Kelly's Last Stand

MAP P.66, POCKET MAP A17
11A Ashley Rd Ⓜ Tsim Sha Tsui, Exit E.
Daily 11.30am–2am.
Australian bar with good beer and
meaty Aussie food, plus great live
jazz after 9pm. A real favourite with
travellers and expats.

Tequila Jack's

MAP P.66, POCKET MAP C17
35 Chatham Rd South Ⓜ Tsim Sha Tsui, Exit
D2. ☎ 3428 5133. Daily 11am–1am.
Small Mexican-inspired watering
hole offering a bar list of
margaritas and imported beers,
plus Tex-Mex chow, a long bar and
pavement tables.

Vibes

MAP P.66, POCKET MAP B16
5/F, The Mira Hong Kong, 118 Nathan Rd
Ⓜ Tsim Sha Tsui, Exit B1 ☎ 2315 5999.
Sun–Thurs 4pm–midnight, Fri & Sat
5pm–1am.
Fifth-floor courtyard lounge-bar
open to the sky; good for an
evening cocktail with chilled-jazz
ambience.

Kowloon: Jordan to Diamond Hill

Kowloon's crowds and shopping ethos continue north of Tsim Sha Tsui into Jordan, Yau Ma Tei and Mong Kok. It's a great area for specialist street markets, most of them – once you get past touristy Temple Street Night Market – very Chinese in theme, with food, jade, pets, flowers and clothes on sale. You can also buy electronic goods at lower prices than in Tsim Sha Tsui, and with less chance of being ripped off. Until the acquisition of the New Territories in 1898, Kowloon ended beyond Mong Kok at Boundary Street, though today it extends a further 3km north to a natural dividing line at the base of the jagged Kowloon Hills. This area beyond Boundary Street is largely residential, with a handful more markets and sights accessible by public transport – including a beautiful traditional garden at Diamond Hill.

Shanghai and Reclamation Streets

MAP P.78, POCKET MAP A10–A15
Ⓜ Yau Ma Tei, Exit B2.

The streets north of Jordan Road are interesting places to browse the low-key businesses which

Shanghai Street

serve locals' daily needs. **Shanghai Street** contains an eclectic and attractive mix of shops and stalls selling items as diverse as bright-red Chinese wedding gowns (at no. 194), embroidered pillow cases, lacquered shrines and other temple accessories (at no. 216), chopping blocks, incense and kitchenware (including a smith selling razor-sharp cleavers at no. 297). To the west, **Reclamation Street** sports an intense produce market between Nanking and Kansu streets, offering concrete proof that the Cantonese demand absolutely fresh food, with fish, frogs and turtles alive in tanks and buckets for shoppers to inspect.

Temple Street Night Market

MAP P.78, POCKET MAP A14
Temple St, Jordan/Yau Ma Tei Ⓜ Jordan.
Daily 5–11pm.

Temple Street Night Market is a fun, noisy, cramped run of stalls selling tourist-oriented knickknacks, electronic goods, and smartphone covers. Another draw is the **alfresco seafood restaurants** north of Saigon Street: a couple of plates of sea snails, prawns and mussels shouldn't be too expensive (though you need to fix prices in advance), and it's a great place to take in the atmosphere. Moving north across Kansu Street, you pass a string of **fortune tellers** who somehow predict the future from the antics of their caged budgies; keep an ear open for a competing pair of karaoke booths, belting out Cantonese folk songs.

By now you're at a square, in the middle of which is the heavy stone **Tin Hau Temple** (daily 8am–5pm; free), named after and dedicated to the southern Chinese sea goddess – and indicating that this was once the local waterfront in the days before land reclamation. Note that Temple Street and the night market continue north from the far side of the square, where you'll also find more places to eat.

Bracelets for sale at the Jade Market

The Jade Market

MAP P.78, POCKET MAP A14
Kansu St, Yau Ma Tei Ⓜ Yau Ma Tei, Exit C. Daily 9am–6pm.
Located under a busy overpass, Yau Ma Tei's **Jade Market** features several hundred stalls selling an enormous selection of jade jewellery, statues and antique reproductions. In part, jade owes its value to the fact that it's a hard stone and very difficult to carve; it's also said by the Chinese to promote longevity and prevent decay (in ancient times royalty used to be buried in jade suits made of thousands of tiny tiles held together with gold wire).

There are basically two kinds of jade: nephrite (which can be varying shades of green), and the rarer jadeite, much of which comes from Burma and which can be all sorts of colours. A rough guide to quality is that the jade should be cold to the touch and with a pure colour that remains constant all the way through; coloured tinges or blemishes can reduce the value. However, unless you know your stuff, the scope for being misled is enormous, so it's more enjoyable to just poke around the stalls to see what turns up for a few dollars. Note that all the serious buying is over before lunch.

The Ladies' and Goldfish markets

MAP P.78, POCKET MAP A10 & B12
Mong Kok Ⓜ Mong Kok, Exit D2. Daily from 10am till after 5pm.
Two interesting markets can be found in Mong Kok's Tung Choi Street. Between Dundas and Shantung streets, the crowded stalls of the **Ladies' Market** mostly sell inexpensive clothing, though you might find better bargains at Sham Shui Po. North of Bute Street, the **Goldfish Market** is one long, crowded run of shops festooned with all kinds of ornamental and tropical fish in tanks and fairground-style plastic bags, as well as the necessary accessories for displaying them at home. Goldfish are a popular symbol of good fortune and wealth

Jordan to Diamond Hill

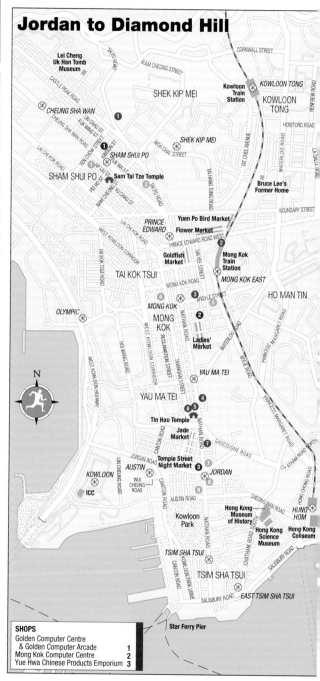

CORNWALL STREET

Lei Cheng Uk Han Tomb Museum

NAM CHEONG STREET

TAI PO ROAD

CASTLE PEAK ROAD

KOWLOON TONG

Kowloon Train Station

KOWLOON TONG

RENFREW ROAD

SHEK KIP MEI

✴ CHEUNG SHA WAN

CHEUNG SHA WAN ROAD

UN CHAU ST

FUK WING ST

HEREFORD ROAD

WATERLOO ROAD

LA SALLE ROAD

TAI CHEUI AVENUE

WOH CHAI STREET

SHEK KIP MEI

LAI CHI KOK ROAD

YEN CHOW STREET

KI LUNG ST

UK WA ST

SHAM SHUI PO ✴

SHAM SHUI PO

AP LIU ST

Sam Tai Tze Temple

TAI HANG TUNG ROAD

Bruce Lee's Former Home

PEI HO ST

NAM CHEONG YU CHAU ST

PAI PO ROAD

BOUNDARY STREET

LAI CHI KOK ROAD

PRINCE EDWARD

WEST KOWLOON CORRIDOR

Yuen Po Bird Market

Flower Market

PRINCE EDWARD ROAD WEST

TAI KOK TSUI ROAD

Goldfish Market

SAI YEE STREET

Mong Kok Train Station

TAI KOK TSUI

MONG KOK ROAD

MONG KOK EAST

HO MAN TIN

✴ OLYMPIC

WEST KOWLOON CORRIDOR

NATHAN ROAD

ARGYLE STREET

MONG KOK

HO WANG ROAD

RECLAMATION STREET

MONG KOK

WATERLOO ROAD

PRINCESS MARGARET ROAD

WEST KOWLOON HIGHWAY

SHANGHAI STREET

Ladies' Market

WYLIE ROAD

YAU MA TEI

YAU MA TEI

NATHAN ROAD

N

Tin Hau Temple

Jade Market

GASCOIGNE ROAD

CH'ATHAM ROAD

PRINCESS MARGARET ROAD

KOWLOON ✴

LIN CHEUNG ROAD

JORDAN ROAD

AUSTIN

Temple Street Night Market

JORDAN

ICC

WUI CHEUNG ROAD

CANTON ROAD

AUSTIN ROAD

HONG CHONG ROAD

Kowloon Park

Hong Kong Museum of History

CHEONG WAN ROAD

✴ HUNG HOM

Hong Kong Science Museum

Hong Kong Coliseum

CHATHAM ROAD SOUTH

TSIM SHA TSUI

CANTON ROAD

KOWLOON PARK DRIVE

NATHAN ROAD

SALISBURY ROAD

EAST TSIM SHA TSUI

SALISBURY ROAD

Star Ferry Pier

SHOPS

Golden Computer Centre & Golden Computer Arcade	1
Mong Kok Computer Centre	2
Yue Hwa Chinese Products Emporium	3

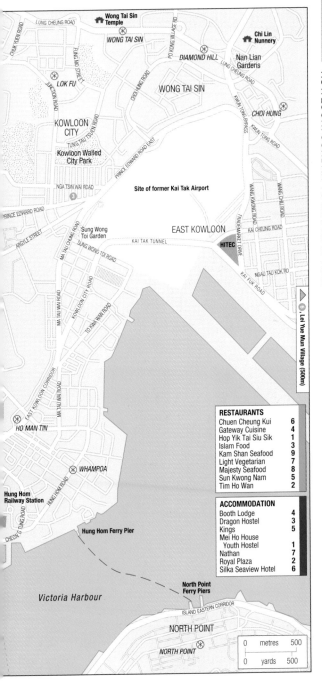

Lei Yue Mun Village (500m)

RESTAURANTS

Chuen Cheung Kui	6
Gateway Cuisine	4
Hop Yik Tai Siu Sik	1
Islam Food	3
Kam Shan Seafood	9
Light Vegetarian	7
Majesty Seafood	8
Sun Kwong Nam	5
Tim Ho Wan	2

ACCOMMODATION

Booth Lodge	4
Dragon Hostel	3
Kings	5
Mei Ho House Youth Hostel	1
Nathan	7
Royal Plaza	2
Silka Seaview Hotel	6

in China (saying "gold fish" in Chinese sounds like saying "gold surplus") and are believed to invoke a trouble-free life; you'll often see drawings of fish or fish-shaped lanterns in temples or on display during Chinese festivals. Consequently, great care is taken with their breeding, and some can cost thousands of dollars.

Flower Market

MAP P.78, POCKET MAP B10
Flower Market Rd, Mong Kok Ⓜ Prince Edward, Exit B1. Daily 10am–6pm.
North of Tung Choi Street and across busy Prince Edward Road, the **Flower Market** Road hosts dozens of inexpensive florists and plant shops, best at the weekends when vendors bring in trucks full of orchids, orange trees and other exotica, crowding the narrow pavements with stalls. Chinese New Year is especially busy with people buying auspicious narcissi, orange trees and plum blossom to decorate their apartments.

Flower Market

Yuen Po Bird Market

MAP P.78, POCKET MAP B10
Off Prince Edward and Flower Market roads, Mong Kok Ⓜ Prince Edward, Exit B1. Daily 7am–8pm.
Mong Kok's **Bird Market** is housed in a purpose-built Chinese-style terrace. There are two or three dozen stalls crammed with caged songbirds, parakeets, mynah birds, live crickets tied up in little plastic bags (they're fed to the birds with chopsticks), birdseed barrels and newly made bamboo cages – minus bird, these start at $100 or so. Little porcelain bird bowls and other paraphernalia cost from around $10. It's interesting just to watch the locals who bring their own caged birds here for an airing and to listen to them sing; taking your songbird out for a walk is a popular pastime among older Chinese men, one you'll see often in parks throughout more traditional areas of Hong Kong.

Sham Shui Po

MAP P.78, POCKET MAP A10

Ⓜ Sham Shui Po.

Northwest of Boundary Street, shabby **Sham Shui Po** is full of **wholesale fashion warehouses** lining central Cheung Sha Wan Road for several blocks. Prices, styles and quantity here outdo Mong Kok's Ladies' Market, while surrounding streets stock haberdashery – fabrics, buttons, ribbon, lace – along with toys and handbags in leather and plastic.

South and parallel with Cheung Sha Wan Road, **Ap Liu Street flea market** (noon until after dark) is where to find all manner of junk and cheap household appliances, from secondhand cameras, power tools and mobile phones to old records from the 1930s, fishing rods and used furniture. As long as you don't expect to unearth anything valuable, it's good fun.

Lei Cheng Uk Han Tomb Museum

MAP P.78, POCKET MAP A10

41 Tonkin St, Cheung Sha Wan Ⓜ Cheung Sha Wan, Exit A3. ☎ 2386 2863, Ⓦ lcsd.gov. hk. 10am–6pm, closed Thurs. Free.

Discovered in 1957 during construction of a housing estate, Lei Cheng Uk's cross-shaped burial chamber dates to the Eastern Han period (25–220 AD) and proves the region was even then under Chinese control. The **Lei Cheng Uk Han Tomb Museum** shows an informative video outlining the excavation of the tomb and the culture that produced it; from here you pass cases of pottery and fragments of bronzeware unearthed at the site to reach the tomb itself, which has been preserved *in situ*. You can't go in, but a glass window gives you a peek at the low-ceilinged, interlocked brickwork. The tomb was presumably built for a local official, though no trace of a body was ever discovered.

Kowloon Walled City Park

MAP P.78, POCKET MAP D10

Tung Tau Tsuen Rd, Kowloon City. Bus #1 from the Tsim Sha Tsui Star Ferry Pier. Daily 6.30am–11pm.

When the New Territories were leased to Britain in 1898, Chinese garrison commanders in Kowloon refused to cede sovereignty, and for the following century Kowloon Walled City remained a self-governing enclave. After WWII, mainland Chinese refugees settled the area and built a high-rise shanty town, which became the haunt of Triad gangs and a no-go area for the police. It took until 1991 to negotiate the Walled City's closure, after which the site was levelled and turned into **Kowloon Walled City Park**. The restored *yamen* (former military headquarters) now houses a photo collection of the Walled City, though the only solid relics of the times are two stone blocks carved with the characters for "south gate", set into an ornamental wall.

Sung Wong Toi Garden (宋王臺花園)

MAP P.78, POCKET MAP D10

Ma Tau Chung Rd. Bus 5C from the Star Ferry terminal, Tsim Sha Tsui. Daily 24 hr.

Sung Wong Toi Garden is another site proving that Hong Kong does have something of a long history. In 1277, the remains of the imperial Song dynasty fled south from the invading Mongol armies to Kowloon, then an uninhabited peninsula at China's southern tip. (Two years later the Mongols triumphed in a sea battle off Lantau Island, during which the last Song prince was drowned.) Their lookout post in Kowloon was a huge granite boulder – later known as *sung wong toi*, the "Song King's Terrace" – which survived intact until the Japanese blew it up to build an airstrip in the 1940s. After World War II, a large fragment was carved in red characters and set up here in this small memorial park, where a plaque explains the whole story.

Lei Yue Mun

MAP P.78

Ⓜ Yau Tong, Exit A2, then a 10min walk.
Overlooking the eastern end of
Victoria Harbour, **Lei Yue Mun**
village is a ramshackle settlement
of low plaster buildings, packed
so close together that overhanging
corrugated iron roofs turn its
narrow lanes into tunnels. At the
far side of the village, an ancient
Tin Hau temple sits among some
large granite boulders, where two
rusting canons point south over the
harbour's narrow neck towards the
Museum of Coastal Defence (see
page 53).

Most people visit Lei Yue Mun
to **eat seafood**, with the village's
fresh-fish shops displaying tanks
of live reef fish, clams, sea snails,
crayfish, cuttlefish and shrimps.
You make your choice from a shop,
where it will be weighed and priced,
then take it to a restaurant to have
it cooked to your instructions. You
pay all bills at the end, so watch out
for scams: fix the price of your fish
before it's bashed on the head, and
the cost of cooking it before it gets
handed to a chef. Restaurants do
open for lunch, but evenings are the
liveliest time to come.

Wong Tai Sin Temple

MAP P.78

Lung Cheung Rd, Wong Tai Sin Ⓜ Wong Tai
Sin, Exit B2. Daily 7am–5pm. Free.
The lavishly decorated **Wong
Tai Sin Temple**, built in 1921,
is dedicated to **Wong Tai Sin**
("Yellow Immortal"), a shepherd
during the Jin Dynasty (265–420
AD) who achieved enlightenment
and became known for his
healing powers. The temple is
Hong Kong's major Taoist
shrine, and some three million
people visit annually to pay their
respects, wish for long life and
have their fortunes told. The
temple's forecourt is lined with
scores of fortune-tellers who
read palms, bumps, feet and
faces; some speak English and
many display testimonials from
satisfied customers.

The main temple building
with its statue of Wong Tai Sin is
often closed, but kneeling crowds
perpetually pack out the front
courtyard, burning incense and
shaking pots full of numbered
bamboo strips known as "fortune
sticks". When one falls out it's
exchanged for a piece of paper
bearing the same number, which
offers a prediction. The busiest days
at the temple are around Chinese
New Year and at Wong Tai Sin's
festival, on the twenty-third day
of the eighth lunar month (usually
in Sept).

Behind the main building is the
Good Wish Garden (Tues–Sun
9am–4pm; $2), with Chinese
pavilions, carp ponds and waterfalls.

Sha Tin Pass

MAP P.78, POCKET MAP D10

Sha Tin Pass Rd, Wong Tai Sin Ⓜ Wong Tai
Sin, then green minibus #18 to Sha Tin
Pass Rd.
Wong Tai Sin Temple sits right
up against the looming **Kowloon
Hills**, from where there are fantastic
views south over the **Sha Tin Pass**.
From the #18 bus stop, follow Sha
Tin Pass Road uphill for a stiff,
forty-minute ascent to the pass –
popular with locals at the weekend
– and once at the wooded top you'll
find toilets, a pavilion and a small
drinks kiosk (closes at 5pm).

Despite the name, the Sha Tin
Pass – or the road, at any rate –
doesn't run on to Sha Tin in the
New Territories, though there is a
footpath in that direction which
lands you near **Tsang Tai Uk** (see
page 90) in around another
ninety minutes. There's also a
marked 1.8km trail to Lion Rock
from the top of Sha Tin Pass Road
– see page 91 for more.

Chi Lin Nunnery

MAP P.78, POCKET MAP D10

Fun Tak Rd, Diamond Hill Ⓜ Diamond Hill,
Exit C2. Daily 9am–4pm. Free.

Nan Lian Gardens

Though only recently founded, **Chi Lin Nunnery** is, uniquely for Hong Kong, built in the ninth-century Tang style, with beautifully proportioned, dark timber buildings arranged around spacious central courtyards. Giant gilded representations of Buddha as the sage Sakyamuni, Manjusri (the incarnation of wisdom) and Samantabadhra (virtue) fill the main hall, whose roof sprouts two upright "horns", a structural necessity to give a gentle curve to the roofline. Side wings contain more statues of Buddhist deities in gold and precious wood – look for a languid one of Avalokitesvara, the original Indian source for Kwun Yam, the Chinese goddess of compassion. The temple is an extremely calming place to visit, joined by a footbridge to the equally tranquil **Nan Lian Gardens**.

Nan Lian Gardens

MAP P.78, POCKET MAP D10
Fun Tak Rd, Diamond Hill Ⓜ Diamond Hill,

Exit C1. Daily 7am–9pm. Free.
Despite being sited in the middle of a ring of busy traffic overpasses, the **Nan Lian Garden** form a delightful oasis. They're screened by trees which block the traffic noise and the sight of soaring apartment blocks outside, and once through the gates you may as well have stepped back over a thousand years into groves of contorted pine trees, dwarf bougainvillea and crepe myrtles, all laid out in the classical Chinese style. Large, oddly shaped rocks evoke landscapes in miniature, while ponds – one full of giant carp, another graced by a stunning gold-painted pavilion, reached via gently arched vermilion bridges – add a sense of space. Several wooden halls around the perimeter are also built to ancient designs; one contains a gift shop, another a gallery and the third displays models of the intricate wooden brackets that support the roofs. The gardens are not especially large, but the layout makes it feel bigger and it's easy to spend an hour strolling around here.

Shops

Golden Computer Centre & Golden Computer Arcade

MAP P.78, POCKET MAP A10

The entire block between Kweilin and Yen Chow streets, Sham Shui Po Ⓜ Sham Shui Po, Exit D2, ahead on the left. Daily 10am–10pm.

Cramped, crowded and mildly seedy palace of computer and electronics accessories on multiple floors. Prices here really are a good deal if you know what you're after, though once-plentiful software pirates have been raided out of business.

Mong Kok Computer Centre

MAP P.78, POCKET MAP B12

Nelson St, between Tung Choi and Fa Yuen streets, Mong Kok Ⓜ Mong Kok, Exit E2 and to the right. Daily 11am–8pm.

Similar to Sham Shui Po's Golden Computer Centre, though closer to the downtown area and without the range or bedrock prices. Still worth a browse if you're after inexpensive electronics and computer parts.

Yue Hwa Chinese Products Emporium

MAP P.78, POCKET MAP B15

301–309 Nathan Rd, Jordan Ⓜ Jordan, Exit A. Daily 10am–10pm.

Longstanding department store specializing in Chinese souvenirs – everything from gift-wrapped medicines and tea to reproduction antique porcelain and massage chairs. Particularly good for clothing and trinkets.

Restaurants

Chuen Cheung Kui

MAP P.78, POCKET MAP B11

33 Nelson St, Mong Kok Ⓜ Mong Kok, Exit E2 ☎ 2396 0672. Daily 11am–11.45pm.

Hakka home-style cooking from China's Guangdong province – the salt-baked chicken, juicy and tender, is a house speciality ($144). Moderate prices make this a popular place with locals, and there's also an English menu.

Gateway Cuisine

MAP P.78, POCKET MAP D10

G/F 58A Praya Rd, Lei Yue Mun Ⓜ Yau Tong ☎ 2727 4628. ⓦ gatewaycuisine.com/eng. Daily 11am–11pm.

The last restaurant at Lei Yue Mun, offering waterfront harbour views and tasty seafood, including razor clams fried with black beans, steamed tiger prawns and soy-steamed scallops. A seven-dish meal costs around $400 a head.

Hop Yik Tai Siu Sik (合益泰小食)

MAP P.78, POCKET MAP A10

121 Kweilin St, Sham Shui Po Ⓜ Sham Shui Po Exit C2 ☎ 2720 0239. Daily 6.30am–8.30pm.

Locally popular and basic hole-in-wall, worth invading for ten minutes to sample their silky-smooth *sheung fan* rice noodles with peanut sauce, skewered *shao mai* dumplings, or fried noodles. Very cheap; around $7 an order.

Islam Food

MAP P.78, POCKET MAP D10

1 Lung Kong Rd, Kowloon City ☎ 2382 2822. Daily 11am–11pm.

Down-to-earth food from northwestern China's Xinjiang province, where the people are mostly Muslim and the food distinctly central Asian. Plump for one of their juicy beef buns, flavoured with spring onion and wrapped in a crispy coating, or "mutton curry" – a spicy lamb stew. Around $75 a head.

Kam Shan Seafood

MAP P.78, POCKET MAP B16

7/F, Chuang's London Plaza, 219 Nathan Rd Ⓜ Jordan, Exit C1 ☎ 2376 3288. Daily 11am–4pm & 6pm–midnight.

Noisy, cheerful place serving excellent fried mantis shrimps, steamed mussels, crispy chilli whitebait, Cantonese roast goose, squid with garlic and crunchy-fried sweet noodles. Mains around $75.

Light Vegetarian

MAP P.78, POCKET MAP B15
G/F, New Lucky House, 13 Jordan Rd Ⓜ Jordan, Exit B2 ☎ 2384 2833. Daily 11am–11pm.
Cantonese vegetarian fare, with everything made out of vegetables, gluten or tofu despite the names: sweet and sour "fish" (taro); a "bird's nest" basket with fried vegetables; and "duck" (marinated, fried beancurd skin packets). Can be overly stodgy if you order the wrong mix of dishes. Mains for around $75 a head.

Majesty Seafood

MAP P.78, POCKET MAP B15
3/F, Prudential Centre, 216–228 Nathan Rd, Jordan Ⓜ Jordan, Exit E ☎ 2723 2399. Daily 7am–midnight, dim sum until 1pm.
Ride the lift to the third floor and settle down, surrounded by fish tanks, for first-rate beef balls, leek dumplings, *char siu* puffs and egg custard tarts in this popular *dim sum* venue. Come prepared for arctic a/c.

Sun Kwong Nam

MAP P.78, POCKET MAP A11
631–633 Shanghai St, Mong Kok Ⓜ Mong Kok, Exit C2 ☎ 2395 0695. Daily 7am–1am.
This Malay-Chinese *cha chaan teng* is a teahouse-fast food joint full of locals, serving Malaysian curries, milky drinks with sago balls, baked pork chops in sweet and sour sauce and trademark Hong Kong "yin-yang coffee" – a mix of tea, coffee and condensed milk.

Tim Ho Wan (添好運點心)

MAP P.78, POCKET MAP A10
9–11 Fuk Wing St, Sham Shui Po Ⓜ Sham Shui Po, Exit B2 ☎ 2788 1226. Mon–Fri 10am–10pm, Sat & Sun 9am–10pm.
Crowds queue round the block to eat at this apparently insignificant place, hungry for their Michelin-star-rated lotus-leaf steamed rice, *char siu* pastries, persimmon cakes and *fun gwor* dumplings. You may wait over an hour for a seat, so it's best to grab a ticket and go shopping.

KOWLOON: JORDAN TO DIAMOND HILL

Dim sum, Majesty Seafood

The New Territories

The New Territories occupy 794 square kilometres between Kowloon and the Chinese border, home to just under half of Hong Kong's inhabitants. Here you'll find self-contained New Towns, built to ease Hong Kong's downtown population pressures, whose modern apartment blocks and shopping malls conceal nineteenth-century temples, fascinating museums, markets and traditional walled villages. Away from these hubs the New Territories are essentially rural, with large parts designated as country parks, offering excellent hiking and coastal walks – especially around the easterly Sai Kung Peninsula. There are also some fun outdoor sights for children, notably the Hong Kong Wetland Park and Kadoorie Farm. With comprehensive rail and bus services, no single destination in the New Territories is beyond the reach of a day-trip from Hong Kong's downtown – which is fortunate, as there's little hotel accommodation out here.

Shing Mun Country Park

MAP P.88
3.5km east of Tsuen Wan Ⓜ Tsuen Wan, Exit B1, then green minibus #82 from Shiu Wo St to Pineapple Dam.

Pineapple Dam, Shing Mun Country Park

Shing Mun Country Park offers an easy two-hour walk around the blue waters of Shing Mun Reservoir. Choose a nice day, take a picnic and expect to see birds, reptiles and **monkeys**.

The bus drops you outside the visitors' centre at the foot of Pineapple Dam, from where a signposted circuit runs clockwise around the reservoir through the shady forest. The best picnic ground is about forty minutes along at the site of a village that was abandoned when the dam was built in 1928 – look for overgrown remains of rice-terrace walls among the trees, proof that this once was an open hillside. Around the tip of the lake (and past a track which climbs, via Lead Mine Pass, to the summit of Tai Mo Shan; see page 87), the trail finally returns to the reservoir's huge dam wall, set above a deep gorge. There's another picnic ground here with tables and benches, and from here

Walled stone building in Kam Tin

it's just fifteen minutes back to the bus stop.

Kam Tin

MAP P.88

Kam Sheung Rd Ⓜ Kam Sheung Road, Exit B and follow signposts for 5min.

Kam Tin township is famous for its outlying walled stone villages, the most visited of which is **Kat Hing Wai** (daily 9am–5pm; $1), which has been inhabited for four hundred years by the Tang clan. The village's iron gates were confiscated during resistance to the British takeover of the New Territories in 1898 and were returned in 1925 after being found in Ireland. Today, Kat Hing Wai is somewhat commercialized, and while the buildings inside the massive encircling wall are very ordinary, the atmosphere is a lifetime removed from Hong Kong's downtown.

About 600m north from here on Shui Tau Road, **Shui Tau Tsuen** village is bigger, and though the protective walls have gone there's a good scattering of old stone temples, narrow lanes and ancestral halls with elegantly carved roofs still standing amid the buildings of a more recent housing estate. Even the modern buildings here reflect the village's original fortified intent, presenting outsiders with security-grilled windows and stark tiled walls.

Tai Mo Shan

MAP P.88

4km north of Tsuen Wan Ⓜ Tsuen Wan West, Exit D, then left to bus depot for bus #51 to the "Country Park" stop at Tsuen Kam Au.

Hong Kong's highest peak at 957m high, **Tai Mo Shan** is nonetheless easy to climb along a vehicle road up the mountain's west face; people come here on cold winter mornings hoping to see frost. The top is often obscured by a smudge of cloud (*tai mo shan* means "Big Hat Mountain"), but on a good day you can see right to Lantau Island and the Chinese border. The walk is very exposed, with no shade most of the way; to catch the sunrise or sunset, consider staying overnight part way up at the basic *Sze Lok Yuen Youth Hostel* (see page 129).

From the **visitors' centre**, follow the picnic ground trail from the

Hong Kong Wetland Park

near the youth hostel. Keep to the main road as it climbs, the scenery getting better with every bend, until you finally reach the summit area. A weather station prevents you from standing on the very top, but the views are just stupendous. Note there's also a trail off the summit down to **Shing Mun Reservoir** (see page 86).

Hong Kong Wetland Park

MAP P.88

Tin Shui Wai Ⓜ Tin Shui Wai, Exit E3 to Light Rail platform, then train #706 to Wetland Park Ⓦ wetlandpark.gov.hk. Daily except Tues 10am–5pm. $30.

Hong Kong Wetland Park covers over half a square kilometre of landscaped saltwater marsh along the Chinese border. The place is so busy with cheerful crowds that you're unlikely to see much wildlife, but it makes a wonderful half-day excursion if you have children to entertain. The park's paths weave

toilet block up steps through dry woodland on to a grassy hillside dotted with huge granite boulders. On the way you'll see docile wild cattle – the descendants of farmed herds – then the path joins the road

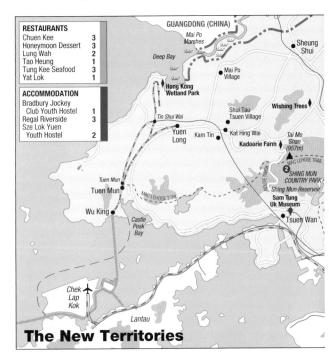

RESTAURANTS	
Chuen Kee	3
Honeymoon Dessert	3
Lung Wah	2
Tao Heung	1
Tung Kee Seafood	3
Yat Lok	1

ACCOMMODATION	
Bradbury Jockey Club Youth Hostel	1
Regal Riverside	3
Sze Lok Yuen Youth Hostel	2

GUANGDONG (CHINA)

Mai Po Marshes

Sheung Shui

Deep Bay

Mai Po Village

Hong Kong Wetland Park

Shui Tau Tsuen Village

Wishing Trees

Tin Shui Wai

Yuen Long

Kam Tin

Kat Hing Wai

Tai Mo Shan (957m)

Kadoorie Farm

MAC LEHOSE TRAIL

ROUTE TWISK

SHING MUN COUNTRY PARK

Shing Mun Reservoir

Tuen Mun

MAC LEHOSE TRAIL

Sam Tung Uk Museum

Wu King

Tsuen Wan

Castle Peak Bay

Chek Lap Kok

Lantau

The New Territories

Hiking trail information

Hiking maps and information for all country parks and trails covered in this chapter can be found online at Ⓦ afcd.gov.hk, under "Country and Marine Parks". English-language bookshops also stock the pocket-sized series, *Hiker's Guide to Hong Kong* by Peter Spurrier, with maps and trail accounts. Remoter country trails are not always well marked, and many are exposed, with little shade in summer, so wear a hat and take plenty of water.

over shallow ponds to **bird hides**, with telescopes trained over the mudflats. You'll see herons and egrets; in November, waders, ducks, camouflaged snipe and – if you're lucky – rare black-faced spoonbills drop in. Other highlights include the mangrove boardwalk, where you can watch mudskippers and fiddler crabs, and the butterfly garden, full of bright flowers and pretty insects. Back inside, the **visitors' centre** has a glassed-in observation deck overlooking ponds, an aquarium with fish and

crocodiles, and tanks full of insects and amphibians.

Lion Rock Country Park

MAP P.88

Access as for Sha Tin Pass (p.80); or Ⓜ **Tai Wai, "Che Kung Miu" exit, then taxi 1km up Hung Mui Kuk Rd to park entrance.** Ⓦ **afcd. gov.hk. Free.**

Lion Rock Country Park covers a forested ridge at the western end of the Kowloon Hills which divide Kowloon from the New Territories. From the Tai Wai side, the trail first climbs in thirty

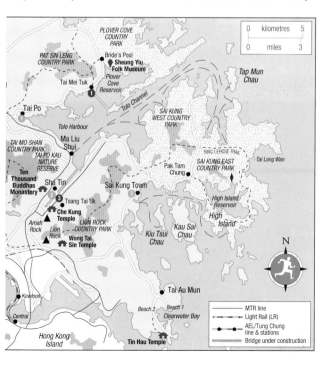

minutes to **Amah Rock**, said to be a woman who turned to stone waiting for her husband to return from fishing. Young women make the pilgrimage up here during the **Maidens' Festival**, held on the seventh day of the seventh lunar month (usually in Aug).

From here, **Lion Rock** is a further hour's hike on a steadily rougher trail, culminating in an easy scramble up to two peaks formed by the lion's "head" and "rump" – on a clear day the views over Kowloon and the harbour are superb. Lion Rock is also a popular spot for **rock climbing**, the best source of information on which is Ⓦhongkongclimbing. com, which provides practical details for a score of routes in Hong Kong, and links to local clubs and climbing centres.

Che Kung Temple

MAP P.88

Ⓜ Che Kung Temple. Follow signs to the temple for 250m. Daily 9am–5pm. Free.

The austere **Che Kung Temple** can be visited en route to Tsang Tai Uk village. Dedicated to the Song Dynasty general **Che Kung**,

who is – among other duties – the god of gamblers, the black-roofed stone building dates to 1993, its entrance marked by a crowd of fortune-tellers, palm readers and incense sellers. Inside, beyond the courtyard, is a 10m-high, aggressive-looking statue of the general with a drawn sword and a collection of brass fans, which people turn for luck.

Che Kung's **festival** is held on the third day of Chinese New Year (in Jan or Feb), when – gambling being so important to the Chinese – the temple is heaving with people coming here to pray for good luck.

Tsang Tai Uk

MAP P.88

Ⓜ Che Kung Temple. Follow signs to the village for 500m. Small donation expected.

Tsang Tai Uk ("The Tsangs' Mansion") is one of the New Territories' lesser-visited walled clan villages, built in the 1870s. Though it is somewhat dilapidated, a visit here provides an insight into how many of the New Territories' families used to live until skyscrapers and freeways began to dominate the area in the

Statue of Che Kung at Che Kung Temple

New Towns

In 1898, when the **New Territories** were first leased to Britain, fewer than ten thousand farmers and fishermen lived in the area. Today, the regional population stands at some 3.7 million, mostly housed in nine **New Towns**. Each **New Town** is designed to be self-sufficient, and for the majority they offer a better environment to live in than the crowded tenement slums of Mong Kok or the outer reaches of Kowloon. Although residential living space in the New Towns is similarly limited, more is provided here in the uncluttered layout of public amenities, civic and leisure services, shops, markets and transport infrastructure.

A look round a New Town gives an insight into the lives of many Hong Kong residents, and what civic planning can achieve in just a few years, given a coherent programme. **Sha Tin** is perhaps the most attractive example, since it's splendidly sited and has had time to acquire a certain character. **Tai Po** is another very liveable example, thanks to the successful blend of new amenities complementing an older, community-oriented town centre, though the New Town's designers don't always get things right: **Tin Shui Wai**, near the Wetland Park, is a horribly anonymous shell of concrete malls and blank-faced residential tower blocks.

1980s. Fortress-like clan villages are a **Hakka** speciality, as these people were dislodged hundreds of years ago by warfare in their homelands in central China, and have never been sure of their welcome in places they subsequently settled. Indeed, *hakka* translates as "guest family", indicating their perpetual status as outsiders.

A triple gateway leads into the village, which includes a central courtyard, wide alleys, a network of high-ceilinged rooms and the clan ancestral hall. The most obvious traditional features are the **four watchtowers** at each corner of the outer wall, whose high, rounded eaves are adorned with spikes to keep bad luck away. The community is very much present, the village's alleyways choked with bicycles, gas canisters, discarded furniture and drying washing.

Sha Tin

MAP P.88, POCKET MAP C10
Ⓜ Sha Tin.

Sha Tin ("Sandy Fields") is a sprawling New Town development

built either side of the Shing Mun River, home to more than half a million people. The town centre is covered by interconnected shopping complexes, of which the massive **New Town Plaza** is the biggest and busiest, packed with restaurants, good-value shops and cruising crowds. Outside, **Sha Tin Park** gives mild relief from the anodyne architecture, with bamboo gardens, a riverside walk and views east over the water to **Lion Rock Park** and Ma On Shan's distinctively hooked peak.

Aside from the **Ten Thousand Buddhas Monastery**, the town's best-known sight is the **Sha Tin Racecourse** (ⓌRacecourse, open race days only; Ⓦsha-tin.com; $10), 3km northeast. It's Hong Kong's second racetrack after Happy Valley, and meetings are held on Wednesday evenings or Saturday and Sunday afternoons during the racing season (Sept–June).

The biggest annual event is the Hong Kong Derby in March, a 2km race for 4-year-olds, which attracts an international crowd.

Hong Kong Heritage Museum

MAP P.88

Man Lam Rd, Sha Tin Ⓜ Sha Tin/
Che Kung Temple and follow signs
Ⓦ heritagemuseum.gov.hk. Mon & Wed–
Fri 10am–6pm, Sat, Sun & public hols
10am–7pm. $20, Wed free.

The **Hong Kong Heritage
Museum** is the SAR's largest
museum, though it's really of more
interest for its temporary shows –
which tend to showcase excellent
and informative collections
of Chinese art and historical
artefacts – than its frankly lifeless
permanent exhibitions. The best
of these is the **Cantonese Opera
Heritage Hall**, full of flamboyant
costumes, embroidered shoes,
stage props and mock-ups of
traditional stage sets. The **Gallery
of Chinese Art** features fine
Chinese ceramics, bronze, jade,
lacquerware and stone sculptures,
while the **New Territories
Heritage Hall** has archeological
remains dating back to 4000
BC, accounts of Hong Kong's
various Chinese ethnic groups,
plus information about ancestral
worship, feasts and festivals.

Ten Thousand Buddhas Monastery

MAP P.88

Ⓜ Sha Tin; exit down the ramp, follow
the road around to the left and take the
first right to the end, where you'll find a
sign and footpath for the monastery. Daily
10am–5pm. Free.

The recently renovated **Ten
Thousand Buddhas Monastery**
dates from the 1960s, and looks
down over Sha Tin from Po
Fook Hill. Four hundred steep
steps ascend to the monastery
from behind the Grand Central
Plaza Shopping Centre, lined by
five hundred life-sized, gilded
statues of Buddhist saints. The
main hall has an undistinguished
exterior but houses thirteen
thousand small black-and-gold
Buddha statues, each sculpted
in a different posture, lining
the walls to a height of 10m or
more. The building also contains
the embalmed and gilded body
of a monk, the founder of the
monastery. Outside on the terrace
there's a pink, nine-storey pagoda,
along with some brightly painted
concrete statues of Chinese deities.
Vegetarian lunches are also

Ten Thousand Buddhas Monastery

available, either from the menu or from a better-value canteen selection.

Tai Po

MAP P.88
Ⓜ Tai Po Market.

The busy New Town of **Tai Po**, which faces east out to sea up the scenic Tolo Channel, is the jumping-off point for the Lam Tsuen Wishing Trees and countryside at **Plover Cove** (see page 93).

Tai Po is all about markets, so head to modern **Tai Po Hui Market** on Heung Sze Wui Street, a five-minute walk from Tai Po Market station. It's a frenetic mix of meat, seafood, vegetables and fruit, with a cooked food centre on the second floor serving inexpensive meals.

North of here, beyond On Fu Road, **Fu Shin Street** is a busy lane of open-air stalls piled with fresh produce, dried seafood and herbs. The granite **Man Mo Temple** halfway along, full of smoke, red brocade and carved wooden altars, was built to celebrate the market's foundation in 1892. Uphill at the southern end of On Fu Road, the **Hong Kong Railway Museum** (Mon & Wed–Sun 10am–6pm; Ⓦ heritagemuseum.gov.hk; free) occupies the unique Chinese-style old station, built in 1913, and is packed with wooden furnishings, model trains and photographs documenting the construction of the original Kowloon-to-Canton Railway. Out the back are coaches and engines from the 1920s to 1950s.

North of the Lam Tsuen River, the town's **Tin Hau Temple** (Ting Kok Road; free) was built around three hundred years ago and reflects Tai Po's former importance as a fishing centre. During the annual **Tin Hau festival** the temple is hung with coloured banners and ribbons, and Cantonese opera performances take place on a temporary stage over the road.

Tai Po Hui Market

Tai Po Kau Nature Reserve

MAP P.88
Green minibus #28K from Kwong Fuk Rd in Tai Po, 2.5km southeast to park gates at Tsung Tsai Yuen bus stop. Daily 8am–5pm. Free.

Tai Po Kau Nature Reserve is a pleasant, thickly wooded area whose colour-coded walking trails take from thirty minutes to over three hours to complete. In the forest there are plenty of butterflies, monkeys and birdlife – especially **sunbirds** and **minivets**, otherwise rare in Hong Kong. Picnic sites at the reserve make this a nice place for an outdoor lunch.

Lam Tsuen Wishing Trees

MAP P.88
Lam Kan Rd. Ⓜ Tai Po Market, then take bus #64K.

The **Lam Tsuen Wishing Trees** are a pair of figs near the roadside southwest of Tai Po, propped up with poles to prevent collapse. People used to write their wishes on paper slips, attach them to a weighted string and hurl them into the branches; but the trees suffered from the weight of accumulated offerings and now wishes are

Pat Sin Leng Country Park

pinned to a nearby notice board. Tourism has boomed here recently, and the site has been marked for massive redevelopment.

Back behind the trees is a pretty **Tin Hau Temple** dating to 1736, and an astounding toilet block, surgically clean and full of piped music and potted orchids. Note that bus #64K continues past Kadoorie Farm to **Kam Tin** (see page 87).

Kadoorie Farm

MAP P.88
Lam Kan Rd. Ⓜ Tai Po Market or Kam Tin, then take bus #64K. Ⓦ kfbg.org. Daily 9.30am–5pm; check opening hours online – it's closed for even minor holidays. $30.
A kilometre west of the Wishing Trees, **Kadoorie Farm** is a working farm specializing in organic and sustainable agriculture, beautifully located on the forested northern slopes of **Tai Mo Shan** (see page 87). Paths lead up through a forested gully and terraced plantations, emerging high up with views north. Kadoorie Farm also serves as a sanctuary for injured and orphaned animals, with muntjac deer, leopard cats, birds of prey and

wild boar on show – probably your one chance to see any of these shy, usually nocturnal animals at close range. There's a small on-site café, plus shelters with picnic tables, so you can bring your own food.

Plover Cove and Pat Sin Leng country parks

MAP P.88
Ⓜ Tai Po Market, then take bus #75K. Ⓦ afcd.gov.uk.
Plover Cove Country Park occupies a rugged east-coast peninsula north of Plover Cove Reservoir, whose dam wall has turned a former marine bay into one of Hong Kong's major water sources. The access point is **Tai Mei Tuk** hamlet, comprising a clutch of food and drink stalls, the *Bradbury Jockey Club Youth Hostel* (see page 129) and a **visitors' centre** (Mon & Wed–Sun 9.30–11.30am & 1.30–4.30pm) providing hiking advice. From here you can follow a trail (or the road) for 5km to **Bride's Pool**, a pretty series of forested waterfalls, popular with picnickers.

Tai Mei Tuk is also the starting point for hikes into **Pat Sin Leng Country Park** – Pat Sin Leng means "Eight Immortals Peak" and the distinct, serrated range is visible from miles away. A 10km trail climbs steeply from behind the visitors' centre to emerge on the ridgetop, which you follow westwards as it continually climbs and descends the short, sharp peaks. About halfway along, **Wong Leng** is the 639m-high apex, and the triangulation point here has fabulous views south and east. At the far end of the trail is **Hok Tau Reservoir** and a sealed road leading to the terminus of green minibus #52B to **Fanling MTR** station. Give yourself eight hours, wear hiking shoes, and take water and a hat.

Clearwater Bay

MAP P.88

Ⓜ Diamond Hill, then take bus #91 (#91R on Sun).

Clearwater Bay is a broad inlet at the New Territories' southeastern extremity. **Tai Au Mun** is the only settlement, boasting two beaches, the small #1 and the much bigger #2, the latter 5km to the south and packed at weekends.

From the bus stop at beach #2, the road and green minibus #16 continue 1500m along a windswept coastline to the members-only Clearwater Bay Golf and Country Club. Steps here descend to a venerable **Tin Hau Temple** on Joss House Bay. As one of the few Tin Hau temples in Hong Kong still facing the sea, this is a major site for annual Tin Hau festivities (see page 142), but is otherwise a quiet, simple structure with a huge terrace at the front to accommodate seasonal crowds. The entrance is guarded by two stone lions: turn the balls in their mouths three times for luck.

Sai Kung town

MAP P.88

Ⓜ Diamond Hill, then take bus #92.

Sai Kung Town

Sai Kung Town is a popular expat haven and a gateway to the wilds of the Sai Kung Peninsula. Small fishing boats sell their catches from the seafront jetty; shoppers hang over the rail to bargain, then their choice is hit on the head and handed up in a basket on the end of a pole. Most visitors take their purchase to one of the waterfront **restaurants**, who cook it according to their instructions – you can also choose from tanks full of live seafood out front. Stalls along the seafront sell tickets for *kaidos* (on-demand ferries) to nearby islands and beaches; pick from a menu of destinations at $30–60 return. The most popular trip is to nearby **Kiu Tsui Chau** (Sharp Island), whose small beach at Hap Mun Bay is one of the prettiest in the area.

The island past Kiu Tsui Chau is the larger **Kau Sai Chau**, with a regular **ferry** (Mon–Thurs 6.40am–7pm & Fri–Sun 6.40am–9pm; every 20 min; $75 return) from its own jetty on the Sai Kung Town waterfront. The main reason to visit is to play golf

Surfers at Tai Wan beach

at the **Jockey Club KSC Public Golf Course** (Ⓦ kscgolf.org.hk for fees and information), the only public course in Hong Kong.

Sai Kung Peninsula

MAP P.88

Ⓦ afcd.gov.hk

The **Sai Kung Peninsula** encompasses 75 square kilometres of rugged headlands, coves, woodland and beaches in Hong Kong's easternmost reaches. Some parts are very wild, but there are also marked paths and quiet places for picnics.

Bus #94 (daily 6.30am–9pm) runs from Sai Kung's bus terminus to the **Pak Tam Chung visitors' centre** (Mon & Wed–Sun 9.30am– 4.30pm; t2792 7365), from where there's a short walking trail to **Sheung Yiu Folk Museum** (Mon & Wed–Sun 9am–4pm; free), at an abandoned traditional walled village. For a longer hike – around eight hours – follow trails via the rim of **High Island Reservoir** to Long Ke Wan, then head north over Sai Wan Hill to the bay at Tai Long Wan.

The best beaches in the area, with white sand and a peacock-blue sea, are at **Tai Long Wan** (Big Wave Bay). The one possible drawback is that it's a lengthy hike to get here, though this also means that not many people make it. Catch **minibus** #29R (Mon–Sat 9.15am, 11.30am & 3.30pm; Sun 11 services 8.30am–4.30pm; $15) to **Sai Wan Ting pavilion** from outside *McDonald's* on Chan Man Street, Sai Kung Town; a taxi costs $95. From the pavilion follow a marked track for an hour, via restaurant shacks at Sai Wan village, to **Ham Tin Wan**, a deep, open beach with another restaurant shack. Immediately north of here is the even longer **Tai Wan beach**; there will be very few people in the vicinity unless a party yacht has pulled in, or your visit coincides with one of Hong Kong's irregular **surfing competitions**.

From Ham Tin Wan, paths head inland again to **Tai Long village** and a long, hot trail back to the main road at **Pak Tam Au**. This is basically a roadside bus stop, with services #94 and #96 heading back to Sai Kung Town.

Restaurants

Chuen Kee

MAP P.88

51–55 Hoi Pong St, Sai Kung Town ☎ 2792 0930. Daily 7am–11pm.

Popular waterfront place offering crab, mantis shrimps, prawns, reef fish and cuttlefish – plus good *dim sum*. Set meals $488 for four dishes.

Honeymoon Dessert

MAP P.88

10 Po Tung Rd (on the highway), Sai Kung Town ☎ 2792 4991. Daily 1pm–2am.

The original of a citywide chain serving desserts made from sago, mango, grass jelly, coconut milk, fruit and ice cream in every conceivable combination. Also famous for their durian concoctions – if you enjoy this heavily-scented fruit, try the durian pancakes.

Lung Wah

MAP P.88

22 Wo Che St, Sha Tin ☎ 2691 1594. Daily 11.30am–10.30pm.

This ancient establishment serves great greasy pigeon – a Cantonese speciality – though it seems to have evaded hygiene regulations. Still, the run-down palatial splendour and strutting caged peacocks are worth a look, even if you choose not to dine.

Tao Heung

MAP P.88

Shop A, Fuller Garden, 8 Chui Lok Street, Tai Po ☎ 2666 9923. Daily 7am–1am.

Main dishes are fairly ordinary, but a great place for *dim sum*: try the white radish cake, roast pork *cheung fan* (stuffed rice noodles) and the beef rissoles with celery.

Tung Kee Seafood

MAP P.88

Waterfront, Sai Kung Town ☎ 2792 7453. Daily 9am–11pm.

This is a cheerful, noisy (and slightly overpriced) place, whose speciality is "bamboo fish": carp, stuffed with preserved turnip, and chargrilled outside on a hand-rotated bamboo pole, at around $200 a head.

Yat Lok

MAP P.88

Po Wah House, Tai Ming Lane, Tai Po ☎ 2656 4732. Daily 11am–11pm.

There's a small English sign in the window of this typical roast-meat restaurant, which was featured in American chef Anthony Bourdain's TV series – but the food here is no better or worse than in many other places in Hong Kong.

Chuen Kee

Lantau

Twice the size of Hong Kong Island, but nowhere near as developed, Lantau has enough sights to merit a couple of full days' exploration. The site of Hong Kong's international airport, it also sports a branch of the Disneyland theme-park franchise, some excellent beaches, a tall peak to hike up and a superb cablecar ride. More traditional offerings include Po Lin Monastery, boasting an enormous seated bronze Buddha statue, old forts at Tung Chung and Fan Lau and the unusual fishing village of Tai O, which is built in part of corrugated iron – about as far from the usual hi-tech image of Hong Kong as it's possible to get. It's easy to visit as a day-trip, but there are also several places here for overnight stays (see page 129).

Hong Kong Disneyland

MAP P.100
Ⓜ Disneyland Ⓦ hongkongdisneyland. com. Daily 10.30am–8pm. $589, children $419.

The world's smallest **Disneyland**, this theme park is worth a visit if you've time to kill between flights, but it's a bit tame compared with Disney's ten other franchises, and queues can also be a drag.

It's split into various zones, including **Main Street USA**, a recreated early twentieth-century mid-American shopping street (though the goods on sale are distinctly Chinese); **Adventureland**, home to Tarzan's treehouse (made of fake bamboo) and a jungle river cruise; **Tomorrowland**, whose excellent rides include a blacked-out rollercoaster; and **Fantasyland**, populated by a host of Disney characters, and whose best feature is Mickey's PhilharMagic 4D film show.

Tung Chung and Ngong Ping 360

MAP P.100
Ⓜ Tung Chung Ⓦ np360.com.hk. Mon–Fri 10am–6pm, Sat & Sun 9am–6.30pm. $145 one-way, $210 return, children $70/100.

Tung Chung is a burgeoning New Town and transport hub close to Hong Kong's International Airport on Lantau's north coast. Its main attraction is the 5.7km, 25-minute-long **Ngong Ping 360 cablecar ride** up the mountainside to Po Lin Monastery and the Big Buddha. Choose a sunny day and the views are truly spectacular, stretching back off Lantau's steep hills, over the airport and out to sea; some people prefer the downward ride, with the landscape feeling as if it's continually falling away. At the top, the touristy village and expensive "Walking With

Hong Kong Disneyland

The Lantau Trail

More than half of Lantau is designated country park, and the circular **Lantau Trail** loops for 70km around its southern half, passing ten campsites and the island's two youth hostels along the way. For detailed information on the trail's twelve stages, including campsite details, check out ⓦ afcd.gov.hk, the Country Parks Authority's website; the *Lantau Trail* leaflet (available at the ferry pier in Mui Wo); or *Hiker's Guide to Hong Kong* by Pete Spurrier, available in English-language bookshops. Don't underestimate the steep, exposed trails – take a hat, sunscreen and water. The 9km section from Mui Wo to Sunset Peak (about 7hr return) gives a good taste of the whole trail: an initially wooded path which climbs to open highlands of thin pasture and stony slopes, with magnificent views down to the coast at every turn. Other good sections are the 10km easy walk (3hr) above the coast between Fan Lau and Tai O, and trails along the south coast (covered on page 101).

Buddha" shows are best skipped in favour of the Po Lin monastery and Big Buddha, just beyond.

Lantau Peak

MAP P.100

The 934m **Lantau Peak**, more properly known as Fung Wong Shan, is the second highest in Hong Kong, and a popular place to watch the sun rise – you can stay the night before at the *S.G. Davis Youth Hostel* (see page 129). The steep 2km trail from Po Lin to the summit takes about an hour to complete, and on a clear day views reach as far as Macau. You can pick up the **Lantau Trail** here and continue 5km (2hr 30min) east to the slightly lower **Tai Tung Shan**, or "Sunset Peak", from where it's a further hour to **Mui Wo** (see page 103).

Lantau Peak

LANTAU

Visiting Lantau

Most people make a **circuit** of Lantau, catching the MTR to Tung Chung, riding the Ngong Ping 360 cablecar to Po Lin, catching a bus down to Tai O and then more buses eastwards, via the south coast beaches, to Mui Wo for the ferry back to Central. **MTR** services operate approximately from 6am to 1am: from Central, it takes 35 minutes to Disneyland and forty minutes to Tung Chung. **Ferries** to Mui Wo, on the island's east coast, depart from the Outer Islands Ferry Piers in Central every thirty minutes between 6.10am and 12.30am. Roughly every third sailing is by ordinary ferry (55min; Mon–Sat $15.90, Sun $23.50), while the rest are fast ferries (40min; Mon–Sat $31.30, Sun $44.90). Buy tickets before you travel from ticket offices at the pier. For **ferry information**, contact Hong Kong and Kowloon Ferry Ltd (☎ 2815 6063, ⓦ nwff.com.hk). Once here, local **buses** connect major sites, as do the island's pale blue **taxis**.

Po Lin Monastery and the Tian Tan Big Buddha

MAP P.100
Ngong Ping. Bus #2 from Mui Wo, #21 from Tai O or #23 from Tung Chung; or cablecar from Tung Chung. Monastery: daily 8am–6pm; Buddha: 10am–5.30pm.

Hidden behind an ornamental stone archway, the **Po Lin Monastery** was founded in 1906 and has grown to be the largest Chan (Zen) Buddhist temple in Hong Kong. The **front hall** sports dynamic carvings of

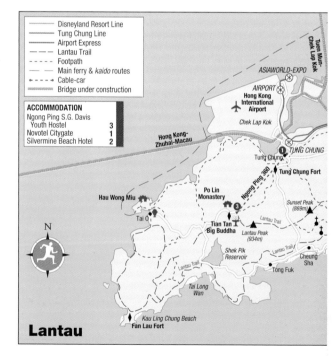

Disneyland Resort Line		
Tung Chung Line		
Airport Express		
Lantau Trail		
Footpath		
Main ferry & *kaido* routes		
Cable-car		
Bridge under construction		

ACCOMMODATION

Ngong Ping S.G. Davis Youth Hostel	3
Novotel Citygate	1
Silvermine Beach Hotel	2

Lantau

phoenixes and coiled dragons, alongside a gilded Buddhist trinity, and opens into the main **Ten Thousand Buddhas Hall**. There's a popular **vegetarian dining hall** (11.30am–4.30pm; set meals $60–100), and much cheaper takeaway **vegetarian *dim sum*** sold outside, which you can eat at the adjacent tables. All this pales into insignificance beside the gigantic **Tian Tan Big Buddha**, at the top of a flight of steps in front of the monastery, surrounded by flying *apsaras* (Buddhist angels). Completed in 1993, the bronze figure seated in a ring of outsized lotus petals is 34m high and weighs 250 tonnes. Before you climb up, stand on the circular **stone platform** facing the staircase; there's an odd harmonic effect here which makes it sound as if you're inside an echoing building, not out in the open. Climb the steps for supreme views

Tian Tan Big Buddha

over the surrounding hills and down to the temple complex.

Tai O

MAP P.100
Bus #1 from Mui Wo, #11 from Tung Chung or #21 from Po Lin Monastery.

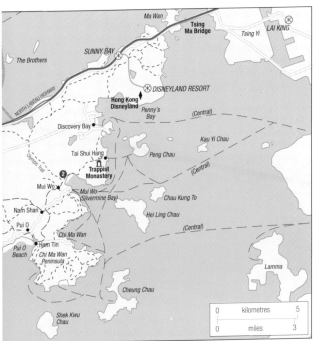

Tai O stilt-houses

prows from a Dragon Boat, a threshing machine and a cutlass. At the bridge, operators offer short **boat trips** (about $50 per person) to see the village from the water and, if you're extremely lucky, **pink dolphins** (see below).

Cross over into the older part of the village and there are a couple of smoky temples worth a quick look. Surrounded by market stalls on the main street, **Kwan Ti Temple** dates to 1500 and honours the god of war and righteousness. **Hau Wong Miu** Temple, on Kat Hing Back Street, was built in 1699 and contains the local boat used in the annual Dragon Boat Races, some shark bones, a whale head and a carved roof-frieze displaying two roaring dragons.

The largest and oldest village on Lantau, **Tai O** is an atmospheric jumble of lanes, shrines and temples, and features a quarter full of tin-roofed stilt-houses built over the water, home to two thousand people. From the bus stop, you cross a small bridge onto the main street, which is lined by people selling dried and live seafood, including foul-smelling shrimp paste, and a refreshing red drink made from begonias. There's also a tiny **museum** (Tues–Sun 12.30–5pm; free) displaying everyday artefacts such as washboards, the

The south coast

MAP P.100

Lantau's best beaches line the **south coast**. All of them are accessible on foot from Mui Wo along the Lantau Trail, or by bus #1 or #2 (to Tai O and Po Lin Monastery respectively from Mui Wo) as far as Shek Pik Reservoir. Closest to Mui Wo is **Pui O beach** (9km; 3hr on foot), an excellent spot with barbecue pits and a free campsite. The next beach along is **Cheung Sha** (5km; 1hr 30min from Pui O on foot), Hong Kong's longest stretch of sand at 2km, partly shaded with casuarina trees and

Pink dolphins

Hong Kong's waters are home to the world's entire population of **pink dolphins** (a subspecies of the Indo-Pacific humpbacked dolphin), currently estimated at sixty animals. Mostly seen off western Lantau, their rapidly declining numbers are thought to be the result of a combination of increasingly polluted waters and over-fishing. Trips to see them are run by Hong Kong Dolphinwatch (☎ 2984 1414, ⓦ hkdolphinwatch.com; 5hr; $460 for adults, $230 for children), part of the profits from which go to the WWF to support dolphin research projects. While the trips could potentially disturb the dolphins, Dolphinwatch believes that the tours form only a tiny amount of local marine traffic, and might increase awareness about these endangered animals.

with several low-key restaurants and bars. Further west, the road strikes inland to the **Shek Pik Reservoir** (13km; 4hr on foot), landscaped to provide picnic areas and walking trails; you can also just glimpse the Tian Tan Big Buddha from here. From Shek Pik there's a walking track (20min) to another shady beach at **Tai Long Wan**, from where you can again pick up the Lantau Trail for 5km (1hr 30min) to **Fan Lau**, an abandoned, overgrown village at Lantau's southwestern headland. Here, the remains of a 1300-year-old rectangular fort overlook a stunning crescent bay and bright green lagoons at the back of beautiful **Kau Ling Chung** beach.

Mui Wo and around

MAP P.100

Mui Wo, also known as Silvermine Bay, is a small residential community surrounding Lantau's ferry port, with a beach, several hiking trails, some pleasant accommodation and restaurants and a major bus terminus. Mui Wo marks the eastern end of the **Lantau Trail** (see page 99), and also the 5.7km **Olympic Trail** to Tung Chung, which passes a waterfall and old villages guarded by abandoned **watchtowers**. Also popular is the three-hour walk north over the hills, via a Trappist monastery, to **Discovery Bay**. Head along the Tung Wan Tau Road to the end, cross the river bridge and follow the bay round to the right. A signpost eventually points up some steps onto the bare hills, with some excellent views along the way over to Hong Kong Island. The Trappist monastery is closed to the public, so follow the road downhill to a signposted path towards Discovery Bay. This New Town is a too-perfect copy of idealized middle-American suburbia, with happy blonde families zipping about in golf carts, and very few Chinese faces. There's a 24-hour **hydrofoil** from Discovery Bay back to Central ($40; 30min), plus buses to the rest of the island.

Mui Wo

Lamma and Cheung Chau

The Hong Kong SAR encompasses some 260-odd islands, the vast majority of which are tiny, barren and uninhabited. After Lantau, Lamma and Cheung Chau are the pick of the bunch, smaller, uncluttered and relatively laidback, though hardly uncharted territory – both had been settled by the Chinese long before the British arrived. One major draw is the beaches, at least for sunbathing – local pollution means that swimming is often not an option (signs in English give levels for the day and state whether swimming is allowed). Lamma and Cheung Chau are also noted for their seafood restaurants and food stalls, while villages offer a slice of traditional Chinese life. If nothing else, the islands are a complete change from downtown; accommodation is available on both of them (see page 130).

Lamma

MAP P.105

Lamma is an elongated fourteen-square-kilometre stretch of land inhabited by five thousand people, with well-marked paths linking its settlements to small beaches, green hilltops and pleasant seascapes. **Yung Shue Wan** is a pretty, tree-shaded village at the northwestern end of the island, where the bulk of Lamma's residents live, and the main ferry terminus. There's a century-old Tin Hau temple here but nothing else to stop you beginning the walk across the island. Twenty minutes along a good concrete path is **Hung Shing Ye**, with a tiny, shaded sand beach with barbecue pits, a couple of places to eat and drink, and unfortunately close views of the power station. The path continues around the beach and up the hill on the other side, before levelling out at a viewing point marked by a Chinese pavilion. Go down the hill, past the vast cement works to your left, to some houses from where side tracks lead to **Lo So Shing**, another beach with changing rooms, showers, a snack kiosk and barbecue pits.

At the end of the main path (around 5km, or 1hr 30min on foot from Yung Shue Wan), is **Sok Kwu Wan**, a fish-farming village and second ferry terminus for Hong Kong Island; floating wooden frames cover the water, interspersed with rowing boats, junks and the canvas shelters of the fishermen and women. There's another Tin Hau temple here by the main pier, along which Sok Kwu Wan's **seafood restaurants** form a line, with outdoor tables overlooking the bay and large fish tanks set back on the street. Some restaurants have English menus, but always ask the price first. Walking tracks link Sok Kwu Wan, via the small village of **Mo Tat Wan**, to spacious **Shek Pai Wan beach** on Lamma's southeastern coast – about an hour's walk in all. There's also a trail from Sok Kwu Wan up to the summit of **Mount Stenhouse**

Visiting Lamma

Ferries to Yung Shue Wan depart from the Outer Islands Ferry Piers in Central (Mon–Sat 6.30am–12.30am, Sun 7.30am–12.30am; 30min; Mon–Sat $17.80, Sun $24.70). **Ferries to Sok Kwu Wan** also depart from the Outer Islands Ferry Piers in Central (daily 7.20am–11.30pm; 25min; Mon–Sat $22, Sun $31). Buy tickets before you travel from the ticket offices at the pier. For **ferry** information, contact Hong Kong and Kowloon Ferry Ltd (🌐 hkkf.com.hk).

(also known as Shan Tei Tong), 353m up in the middle of the island's southwestern bulge – it's a two-hour hike each way.

Cheung Chau

MAP P.106

Cheung Chau ("Long Island") was the stronghold of the Qing dynasty pirate Cheung Po Tsai. Along with his forty thousand followers, he terrorized shipping and villages along the adjacent Chinese coast, reputedly hiding his booty in a cave at Cheung Chau's southern end. After surrendering to government forces in 1810, he was appointed head of the local Chinese navy.

Today, Cheung Chau is the most densely populated of the outlying islands and packed to bursting with day-trippers at weekends and holidays; the main attractions are the beach, watching the thriving traditional life in the main village, with its fishing boats and stalls, and – as ever – sampling the local seafood.

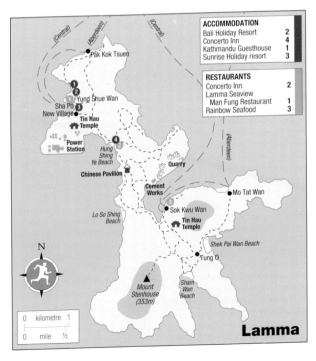

ACCOMMODATION	
Bali Holiday Resort	2
Concerto Inn	4
Kathmandu Guesthouse	1
Sunrise Holiday resort	3

RESTAURANTS	
Concerto Inn	2
Lamma Seaview	
Man Fung Restaurant	1
Rainbow Seafood	3

Pak Kok Tsuen

Yung Shue Wan

Sha Po New Village

Tin Hau Temple

Power Station

Hung Shing Ye Beach

Chinese Pavilion

Quarry

Cement Works

Sok Kwu Wan

Tin Hau Temple

Mo Tat Wan

Lo So Shing Beach

Shek Pai Wan Beach

Tung O

N

Mount Stenhouse (353m)

Sham Wan Beach

| 0 | kilometre | 1 |
| 0 | mile | ½ |

Lamma

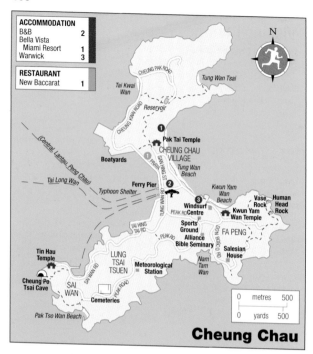

ACCOMMODATION
B&B — 2
Bella Vista
Miami Resort — 1
Warwick — 3

RESTAURANT
New Baccarat — 1

Cheung Chau

Ferries dock at **Cheung Chau Village**, where the island's population and activity is concentrated. The waterfront road hosts a large daily market (busy all day), where fishermen, fruit-and-veg sellers and cultivated-pearl traders rub shoulders. Just beyond the pier, down Tung Wan Road, you'll see an ancient banyan tree, whose base is often cluttered with makeshift altars.

One block in from the water on San Hing Street, the Pak Tai **Temple** (free) is dedicated to the "Northern Emperor", protector against floods. Inside is an 800-year-old iron sword believed to bring luck to fishermen, and a gilded sedan chair, for carrying the god's statue during festivals. The temple is the venue for the vibrant annual four-day **Cheung Chau Tai Chiu Bun Festival**, held to placate the vengeful spirits of those killed by Cheung Chau's pirates (see page 142). North of the village, various paths lead up to a hilltop reservoir and views over the whole island.

From the village, crossing east over the narrow middle of the island lands you at the long **Tung Wan beach** and, around the southern headland, **Kwun Yam Wan beach**, the best on the island. Alternatively, for a two-hour walk from the village, follow the shore southwest from the ferry pier to a pavilion overlooking the harbour and a landscaped picnic area. Behind this is a side path down between the rocks on to a small rocky beach and up to a headland covered in large, rounded granite boulders, which has some superb views over the sea on a calm day.

The path continues down to **Pak Tso Wan beach** – small and sandy, though a little grubby – and then into the shady lanes on the village outskirts, which you can follow northeast to Kwun Yam Wan beach.

Visiting Cheung Chau

Ferries to Cheung Chau depart from the Outer Islands Ferry Piers in Central (daily 24hr; 40–55min; ordinary ferry Mon–Sat $13.20, Sun $19.40; fast ferry Mon–Sat $25.80, Sun $37.20).

Buy tickets before you travel from ticket offices at the pier. For **ferry information**, contact the New World First Ferry Company (W nwff.com.hk).

Restaurants

Most of the following open daily mid-morning and close by 9pm. At alfresco businesses, agree on prices when ordering to avoid being ripped off.

Concerto Inn

MAP P.105

Hung Shing Ye beach, Lamma ☏ 2982 1668, W concertoinn.com.hk. Daily 10am–9pm (last orders 8pm).

Near a small and quiet beach, this hotel-restaurant is set on a delightful terrace and serves an eclectic range of southeast Asian dishes. Mains from $180.

Lamma Seaview Man Fung Restaurant

MAP P.105

Near the pier, Yung Shue Wan, Lamma ☏ 2982 0719. Daily 10am–10pm.

Fresh crab, abalone, fish from live tanks and a long list of budget rice and noodle dishes are on the menu here, served at outdoor tables under beach umbrellas, offering pleasant views while you enjoy your meal.

New Baccarat (新金湖)

MAP P.106

Cnr of Pak She 4th Lane, 150m north from the ferry, Cheung Chau. Daily 10am–10pm.

Simple waterfront restaurant with tables under an awning, serving stir-fried razor clams, prawns and fish (from $80). Set meals $188 for 3 dishes.

Rainbow Seafood

MAP P.105

23–25 First Street, Sok Kwu Wan, Lamma ☏ 2982 8100, W rainbowrest.com.hk. Mon–Fri 11am–10pm, Sat & Sun 10.30am–10pm.

At this place you're invited to pick your fresh seafood directly from the tank. Along with lightly steamed whole fish, there's masterful deep-fried squid with chillies and salt. Slightly overpriced, with set menus for two from $400.

Cheung Chau Bun Festival

Macau

Sixty kilometres west from Hong Kong across the Pearl River delta – and soon to be connected by a $15 billion bridge – the former Portuguese enclave of Macau occupies a 26-square-kilometre peninsula and two artificially fused islands jutting off the Chinese mainland. With well-preserved colonial architecture and Portuguese-influenced cuisine, Macau's European heritage is more obvious than Hong Kong's, though the majority of the population is Chinese. Millions of tourists flock here each year, primarily to gamble at Macau's casinos – it's the only place in China where they have been legalized. Downtown Macau comprises a packed old quarter of forts, temples, churches and narrow streets, alongside a modern casino strip. South from the peninsula across three long, ribbon-like bridges, Taipa and Coloane are conjoined islands with more outrageous casinos and a spacious black-sand beach.

Largo do Senado

MAP P.110, POCKET MAP E11

Largo do Senado (Senate Square) is Macau's public focus, cobbled and surrounded by elegant colonial buildings painted pale pink, yellow or white, with shuttered upper storeys and street-level colonnades. **Leal Senado**, the Senate House itself (daily 9am–9pm; free), faces Largo do Senado on Avenida de Almeida Ribeiro. It's of traditional Portuguese design, featuring classic blue-and-white *azulejo* tiling, an ornamental courtyard out the back, and an impressive upstairs library (Mon–Fri 1–7pm), with many old books about China. The adjacent Senate Chamber – a grand room with panelled walls and ceiling and excellent views over the square – is open to the public when not being used for official functions.

West off Largo do Senado, down Rua de São Domingos and adjacent streets, is a bustling **produce market**, surrounded by stalls selling inexpensive clothing. On the opposite side of the square is **Santa Casa de Misericordia** (Tues–Sun 10am–1pm & 2.30–5.30pm; MOP$5), a charitable institution which was founded in 1569 by Dom Belchior Carneiro, Macau's first Catholic bishop (whose skull is displayed in a wood-panelled museum upstairs).

Money in Macau

Macau's currency is the pataca (MOP$), divided into avos. Coins come in 10, 20 and 50 avos denominations, notes in 10, 50, 100 and MOP$1000. The Hong Kong dollar and pataca are almost equal in value; you can use Hong Kong dollars in Macau but not pataca in Hong Kong.

Macau Light Rail

Macau currently has a **light rail** system under construction. Due for completion between 2019– 2020, it will circuit the peninsula and Cotai district, connecting the ferry terminals, airport and border crossing points.

East off Largo do Senado, Travessa da Sé slopes uphill to a smaller cobbled square and the squat and undistinguished **Sé** (daily 9.30am–6pm; free), Macau's cathedral, last rebuilt in 1937 and featuring some fine stained glass. Just past here, **Lou Kau Mansion** (Tues–Sun 10am–6pm; free) is a fabulous two-storey Chinese merchant's house, built in 1889, sporting a central atrium and beautiful wooden furnishings.

Back at Largo do Senado and moving north, the arcaded buildings peter out in the adjacent Largo São Domingos, which holds Macau's most beautiful church, the seventeenth-century Baroque **São Domingos** (daily 10am–6pm; free). Its cream-and-stucco facade is echoed inside by the pastel-coloured pillars and walls, and by a quiet statue of the Virgin and

Child. On May 13 every year the church is the starting point for a major procession in honour of Our Lady of Fatima.

São Paulo

MAP P.110, POCKET MAP E11

North of São Domingos, through a nest of cobbled lanes flanked by *pastelarias* (shops selling sweets, biscuits and roast meats), stands the imposing facade of **São Paulo** church. Founded in 1602, its rich design reflected the cosmopolitan nature of early Macau – designed by an Italian in a Spanish style, and built by Japanese craftsmen. São Paulo became a noted centre of learning until the expulsion of the Jesuits from Macau, after which it became an army barracks. In 1835 a fire, which started in the kitchens, destroyed the entire complex except for the carved

São Paulo facade

stone front. On approaching up the wide swathe of steps it seems at first that the church still stands, but on reaching the terrace the facade alone is revealed, like a theatre backdrop, rising in four chipped and cracked tiers. The symbolic statues and reliefs include a dove at the top (the Holy Spirit) flanked by the sun and moon.

Fortaleza do Monte

MAP P.110, POCKET MAP E12
Daily 7am–7pm. Free.

East of São Paulo the solid **Fortaleza do Monte**, once part of the São Paulo complex, saw action only once, when its cannons helped repel the Dutch in 1622. The ramparts, lined with the weathered cannons, give views over almost the whole peninsula.

The fort houses the **Museu de Macau** (Ⓦmacaumuseum.gov.mo, Tues–Sun 10am–6pm; MOP\$15). The first floor charts the arrival of

the Portuguese and the heyday of the trading routes, with displays of bartered goods (wooden casks, porcelain, spices, silver and silk). The second floor has more of a Chinese theme, with full-sized street reconstructions as well as footage of customs and festivals. Offbeat items include a display on cricket-fighting (where two of these aggressive insects are pitted against each other), complete with a tiny coffin and headstone for expired fighters.

Hong Kung Temple

MAP P.110, POCKET MAP E11
Rua Cinco de Outubro.

The unpretentious **Hong Kung Temple** is dedicated to Kwan Tai, god of riches and war, and is the focus for the extraordinary **Drunken Dragon Festival**, held on the eighth day of the fourth lunar month (April or May). Organized by the Fish Retailers'

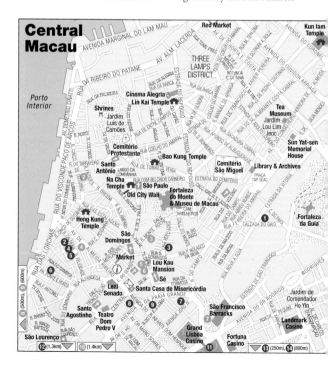

Association, the festival features opera, religious ceremonies, martial arts performances and a parade from here to the Porto Interior (Inner Harbour) via all the local fish shops, by men carrying large wooden dragon heads and consuming vast quantities of spirits.

Jardim Luís de Camões

MAP P.110, POCKET MAP E11
Praça Luís de Camões. Daily 6am–10pm. Free.

The **Jardim Luís de Camões** (Camões Garden) is a very tropical, laidback spread of banyans, ferns, fan palms, paved terraces and flowers. It's always full of people pottering about, exercising or playing cards under the trees, and commemorates the sixteenth-century Portuguese poet who is supposed to have visited Macau and written part of his epic *Os Lusíadas* (about Vasco da Gama's voyages) here. There's a bust of Camões,

Cemitério Protestante

encircled by granite boulders, although there's no concrete evidence that he ever came here.

Cemitério Protestante

MAP P.110, POCKET MAP E11
Rua de Entre Campos. Daily 8.30am–

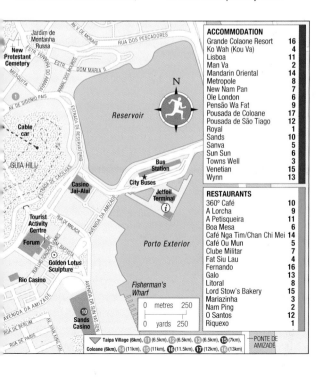

ACCOMMODATION	
Grande Coloane Resort	16
Ko Wah (Kou Va)	4
Lisboa	11
Man Va	2
Mandarin Oriental	14
Metropole	8
New Nam Pan	7
Ole London	6
Pensão Wa Fat	9
Pousada de Coloane	17
Pousada de São Tiago	12
Royal	1
Sands	10
Sanva	5
Sun Sun	6
Towns Well	3
Venetian	15
Wynn	13

RESTAURANTS	
360° Café	10
A Lorcha	9
A Petisqueira	11
Boa Mesa	6
Café Nga Tim/Chan Chi Mei	14
Café Ou Mun	5
Clube Militar	7
Fat Siu Lau	4
Fernando	16
Galo	13
Litoral	8
Lord Stow's Bakery	15
Mariazinha	3
Nam Ping	2
O Santos	12
Riquexo	1

Jardim de Montanha Russa
New Protestant Cemetery
AV. V. DE MORAIS
RUA DOS PESCADORES
ESTR. FERREIRA DO AMARAL
RAMAL DOS MOUROS
DOM MARIA
MESQUITA
AV. DE SIDONIO PAIS
ESTRADA DE RESERVATORIO

Reservoir
N

Cable car

GUIA HILL
ESTRADA DE CACILHAS
Casino Jai-Alai
Bus Station
City Buses
Jetfoil Terminal

Tourist Activity Centre
Forum
RUA DE MALACA
AVENIDA DA AMIZADE
RUA DE BRAGA
RUA DE S. BAPTISTA

Golden Lotus Sculpture
Rio Casino
Porto Exterior
AVENIDA DA SUN YAT-SEN
AVENIDA DA AMIZADE

Fisherman's Wharf
0 metres 250
0 yards 250

Sands Casino
RUA DE BERLIM
AVENIDA DA AMIZADE
AV. XANG HAG
RUA DE PARIS

PONTE DE AMIZADE

Taipa Village (6km), ⑪ (6.5km), ⑫ (6.5km), ⑬ (6.5km), ⑭ (7km), Coloane (6km), ⑭ (11km), ⑮ (11km), ⑯ (11.5km), ⑰ (12km), ⑱ (13km)

Visiting Macau from Hong Kong

By road

The 55km-long bridge between Hong Kong airport and Macau is due for completion in late 2018. It's not clear how this will affect access, but it's worth asking about direct buses.

By sea

Ferries to Macau's main Outer Harbour Jetfoil Terminal depart the Shun Tak Centre, Sheung Wan, Hong Kong Island (daily 24hr; 1–4 hourly; Ⓦ turbojet.com.hk) and the China Ferry Terminal, Canton Road, Tsim Sha Tsui (daily 7.30am–10.30pm; 15 daily; Ⓦ turbojet.com.hk). Note that some ferries from Hong Kong Island arrive at the Taipa Ferry Terminal, next to Macau's airport. All ferries take 55 minutes and cost about HK$171 each way, though prices rise at weekends. It's advisable to book in advance; buying a return ticket saves time at the other end. Aim to be at the ferry terminal at least thirty minutes before departure to clear customs. Excess luggage – more than a backpack or suitcase – costs $20–40.

By air

A helicopter service to Macau's Jetfoil Terminal operates from the Shun Tak Centre on Hong Kong Island (daily 10am–10.30pm; 1–2 hourly; Ⓦ skyshuttlehk.com). The journey takes fifteen minutes and costs HK$4300 one-way. In Hong Kong, buy tickets from the window adjacent to the ferry ticket office in the Shun Tak Centre; in Macau, tickets are sold from marked booths at the Jetfoil Terminal.

5.30pm. Free.

The **Cemitério Protestante** (Old Protestant Cemetery) houses many of the non-Portuguese traders and visitors who expired in the enclave. For decades, Protestants had no set burial place in Macau: the Catholic Portuguese didn't want them and the Chinese objected if they were interred on ancestral lands. Some of the graves were moved here from various resting places outside the city walls, as the pre-1814 headstones show, and now sit slightly forlornly and somewhat overgrown in this sprawling plot.

The most famous resident is the artist **George Chinnery**, who died here in 1852 having spent his life in India and the Far East recording the development of European trade in the region. Some of the cemetery's most poignant graves are those belonging to ordinary seamen: Samuel Smith "died by a fall from aloft"; a cabin boy similarly met his end "through the effects of a fall into the hold"; while Oliver Mitchell "died of dysentery". The grave of the missionary Robert Morrison, who translated the Bible into Chinese, is also here, as is that of his wife, who died in childbirth.

Jardim Lou Lim Ioc

MAP P.110, POCKET MAP F11
Av. do Conselheiro Ferreira de Almeida.
Daily 6am–9pm. Free.

A high wall encloses the beautiful **Jardim Lou Lim Ioc**, a formal arrangement of pavilions, carp ponds, bamboo groves and frangipani trees. Built in the nineteenth century by the wealthy Chinese merchant Lou Kou, it was modelled on the famous classical Chinese gardens of Suzhou, and typically manages to appear much more spacious than it really is. Jardim Lou Lim Ieoc and Hong Kong's **Nan Lian Gardens** (see page 83) are the only such examples in Hong Kong and Macau. The galleries lining the east side host occasional amateur opera performances on Sundays, and a **tea museum** (free), though captions are in Chinese only.

Guia Hill

MAP P.110, POCKET MAP F11
Av. Sidónio Pais. Daily 6am–8.30pm.
Guia Hill, Macau's apex and site of its former defence headquarters, is now a landscaped park. Paths wind to the top from the entrances on Estrada da Vittoria and Avenida Sidónio Pais; from the latter, there's also a cablecar link to the top (Tues–Sun 8am–6pm; MOP$2

one-way, MOP$3 return). Either way, you'll end up a short walk from the remains of **Fortaleza da Guia** (daily 9am–6pm; free), a fortress completed in 1638, originally designed to defend the border with China, though it's seen most service as an observation post due to its high position. There is a network of short, disconnected tunnels used in the 1930s to store munitions, and a small seventeenth-century chapel within the walls dedicated to Our Lady of Guia. This contains an image of the Virgin – whom local legend says left the chapel and deflected enemy bullets with her robe during the Dutch attack of 1622 – and original blue and pink frescoes, which combine Chinese elements with Christian religious images. The chapel's other function was to ring its bell to warn of storms, something now taken care of by the fortress's lighthouse, built in 1865. The best views from the fortress walls are southeast down

Jardim Lou Lim Ioc

Red Market, Three Lamps District

over the modern Porto Exterior, and westwards towards Fortaleza do Monte and the old town.

Kun Iam Temple

MAP P.110, POCKET MAP F12
Av. do Coronel Mesquita. Daily 7.30am–5pm. Free.

Entered through a banyan-planted courtyard crowded with fortune-tellers, the scruffy, 400-year-old **Kun Iam Temple** is dedicated to the Bodhisattva of mercy (known in Hong Kong as Kwun Yam), and was the venue for the signing of the first ever **Sino-American treaty** on July 3, 1844 by Viceroy Tai Yeng and the US Commissioner Caleb Cushing. The buildings are of the usual heavy stone, but their roofs are decked in colourful porcelain statuettes depicting folk tales and historical scenes. Inside the third hall are statues of Kun Iam and eighteen other **Bodhisattvas**, those who had attained the right to enter paradise but chose to stay on earth to help humanity.

Lin Kai Temple and around

MAP P.110, POCKET MAP E11
Travessa da Corda, off Estrada do Repouso.
Daily 7.30am–5.15pm. Free.

Tucked down a side lane off main Estrada do Repouso, **Lin Kai Temple** is a maze of small halls dedicated to a host of local deities, including the Fire God, Ua Kwong, whose festival is held on the 28th day of the ninth lunar month (some point in Oct). The temple is old, shabby and in need of attention, but it oozes character and there's a small bric-a-brac **night market** outside at the weekends. Just a few doors up on Estrada do Repouso, the little green and white **Cinema Alegria** still has its original 1950s Art Deco fittings, making it an atmospheric place to catch the latest Hollywood or Chinese blockbuster in Cantonese.

Three Lamps District and the Red Market

MAP P.110, POCKET MAP F11
Rotunda de Carlos da Maia.

A few minutes' walk from the Lin Kai Temple, a roundabout marks the centre of the pedestrianized Sam Jan Dang or **Three Lamps District**. The streets immediately north of here are packed with busy market stalls selling bedding, fabrics, fresh produce and – especially – **clothes**; bargain hard and don't believe any marked sizes. Hidden away here is the bizarre **Cheoc Lam Temple**, walled with green tiles, planted with bamboo and again divided into a host of ancestral halls and shrines to an impartial mix of Buddhist and Taoist saints.

There's more activity just north again inside the **Red Market**, another Art Deco building at the intersection of Avenida de Horta e Costa and Avenida do Almirante Lacerda. Designed in 1936 by local architect Jio Alberto Basto, it houses a produce market full of slabs of meat and frozen seafood along with live chickens, pigeons, ducks, fish, frogs and turtles, all waiting to be carted off for dinner.

The Lin Fung Temple and Museu Lin Zexu

MAP P.110, POCKET MAP F10
Av. do Almirante Lacerda.

About 500m north of the Red Market, the **Lin Fung Temple** (daily 7am–5pm; free) was established in 1592 to provide accommodation for travelling officials. It's full of gaudy woodwork painted gold and red, coloured wall mouldings of fantastic beasts and very fine stone carvings above the entrances depicting moral operatic scenes. The temple is dedicated to **Kwan Tai**, a loyal general during the turbulent Three Kingdoms period (around 184–280 AD), who chose to be executed rather than betray his oath brothers. A statue of a horse in the right-hand entrance is a memorial to Kwan Tai's lightning-fast steed **Red Hare**, who pined away and died after his master's execution – people often place vegetables in the statue's mouth.

Off the temple's forecourt, **Museu Lin Zexu** (Tues–Sun 9am–5pm; MOP$5) commemorates another upstanding official, **Lin Zexu** (or Lam Kung), who tried to stamp out the nineteenth-century opium trade by destroying British supplies of the drug, only to be blamed for precipitating the first Opium War and exiled to China's northwest. The museum displays a staid collection of period artefacts, though the account books for 1830–1839 show that the opium trade cost the Chinese treasury between seven and eight million silver pieces annually, amply illustrating why the Chinese court was keen to stop it – and why British traders and local Chinese merchants wanted to keep it going.

The border

MAP P.110, POCKET MAP E10–F10
Bus #5 from the Lin Fong Temple runs a kilometre north to the **border with China**, past an escalation of shops and backstreet markets selling all the things you might have forgotten to buy – or never even realized were for sale – during your stay. Many of the people here are mainland Chinese, buying powdered milk in bulk for resale north of the border.

Lin Fung Temple

Casinos

Macau's 45 **casinos** are frenetic and packed places, some with little padding to their primary function as gambling halls, while an increasing number, like the Grand Lisboa or the Venetian in Cotai, are absurdly ostentatious.

Games on offer include one-armed bandits or slot machines (called "hungry tigers" locally), card games like baccarat and blackjack, and some peculiarly Chinese options: *boule* is like roulette but with a larger ball and fewer numbers; *pai kao* is Chinese dominoes; *fan tan* involves a cup being scooped through a pile of buttons which are then counted out in groups of four, bets being laid on how many are left at the end of the count; and *dai-siu* ("big-small") bets on the value of three dice either having a small (3–9) or big (10–18) value.

Entry is conditional on your being over 18 years old, not wearing shorts, sandals or slippers, handing over bags and cameras at the door and carrying a valid passport. Minimum bets are usually MOP$100.

The only historical monument of any sort is the old stone archway of the **Portas do Cerco** ("Siege Gate", though referred to in English as the Barrier Gate), which has stood in this spot, more or less, since 1849, though now made redundant by the huge modern border terminal behind. There's not really any reason to be here unless you're

Grand Lisboa casino

crossing into China at Zhuhai, in which case – assuming you already have your visa – just follow the crowds into the terminal. If you're just arriving, join the similar hordes streaming south to waiting taxis and casino buses (the public bus station is underground).

Rua da Felicidade

MAP P.110, POCKET MAP E12

On the west side of the southern peninsula is the **Porto Interior** or Inner Harbour, formerly Macau's main port area. Between here and the **Leal Senado** (see page 108) is a warren of backstreets. The most interesting is **Rua da Felicidade** (Happiness Street). This was once a sordid red-light district but now – even though prostitutes linger – it comprises an atmospheric run of guesthouses, *pastelarias* selling biscuits and cured pork, and restaurants; the shop fronts have all been whitewashed, and their shutters and big wooden doors restored and painted red.

The Barra

MAP P.110, POCKET MAP E12

The Barra is the district at the southern end of Macau's peninsula, cut by Rua Central and its continuations, a dense collection of nineteenth-century civic buildings and cheap Chinese cafés, clothes-making workshops and small businesses. On Rua Central, the peppermint-coloured **Teatro Dom Pedro V** (Mon & Wed–Sun 10am–6pm; free) dates to 1873; opposite is the contemporary church of **Santo Agostinho**. Further south, the square-towered **São Lourenço** church is framed by palms and fig trees, its interior decorated in wooden panels depicting the Stations of the Cross. Above, on Penha Hill, a stiff walk is rewarded by the nineteenth-century **Bishop's Palace and Penha Chapel** (daily 10am–5pm; free); the exteriors are drab, but views south of the bridges snaking over to Taipa compensate.

Back down below, **Rua do Padre Antonio** crosses tiny **Largo do Lilau**, a residential square where a spring seeps out of a wall-fountain. This was one of the first areas of Macau to be settled, and older buildings include a **Mandarin's House** from 1881 on Travessa Antonio da Silva (Mon, Tues & Thurs–Sun 10am–6pm; free), a whitewashed complex of Chinese halls and courtyards. From here the main road becomes **Calçada da Barra**, and 500m south brings you to the yellow and white arched colonnade surrounding the **Quartel dos Mouros** (Moorish Barracks; daily 9am–6pm), built in 1874 to house a Goan regiment and now home to the Port Office. The lobby

A-Ma Temple

has an unlikely collection of naval cannon and ceremonial pikestaffs. From here, it's a couple of minutes downhill to the A-Ma Temple.

A-Ma Temple

MAP P.110, POCKET MAP E12
Rua do Almirante Sérgio. Daily 7am–6pm. Free.

The **A-Ma Temple** is Macau's oldest place of worship, founded in 1370 and named after a girl whose spirit would appear to save people at sea (known in Hong Kong as Tin Hau and elsewhere in Southeast Asia as Mazu). When the Portuguese made their first landfall here in the early 1550s, they unintentionally named the whole territory after her ("Macau" being a corruption of *a ma kok*, the name of the headland). Rebuilt after a fire in 2016, complex comprises a series of small stone halls and pavilions jumbled together on the hillside among granite boulders, all cluttered with incense spirals and red-draped

Land reclamation

Land reclamation has seen the Macau peninsula grow three times bigger over the last 150 years. Part of an accompanying drive for modernization, the biggest development projects so far include the expansion of the Porto Exterior area, the southern peninsula's waterfront being closed up to form two artificial lakes, and the fusing together of the former islands of Taipa and Coloane. A positive aspect of this land reclamation is that the older parts of town haven't been targeted for wholesale demolition – something all too common on the Chinese mainland.

wooden models of boats and statues of the goddess. Several rocks are also carved with symbols of the A-Ma story and poems in Chinese, describing Macau and its religious associations. There is also an array of fish tanks full of turtles, onto whose shells people aim to drop coins for good luck. The busiest time to visit is for the **A-Ma Festival** (the 23rd day of the third moon, April or May; see page 142).

Museu Marítimo

MAP P.110, POCKET MAP E12
Rua do Almirante Sérgio. Ⓦ marine.gov.
mo. Mon & Wed–Sun 10am–6pm. MOPS10.
Macau's **Museu Marítimo** (Maritime Museum) is an engaging and well-presented collection relating to local fishing techniques and festivals, Chinese and Portuguese maritime prowess, and boat-building. There's navigational equipment, a scale model of seventeenth-century Macau, traditional clothing used by the fishermen, a host of lovingly made models of Chinese and Portuguese vessels, and even a small collection of boats moored at the pier. These

include a wooden *lorcha* – used for chasing pirate ships – and racing craft used during the **Dragon Boat Festival** (see page 143). The whole collection is made eminently accessible with the help of explanatory English-language notes and video displays.

Fortaleza de São Tiago da Barra

MAP P.110, POCKET MAP E12
Pousada de São Tiago, Rua São Tiago da Barra.
Set at Macau's southernmost tip, the **Fortaleza da Barra** was once Macau's most important fortress. Completed in 1629, it was designed with 10m-high walls and lined with cannons to protect the entrance to the Inner Harbour, then just offshore (though land reclamation has converted it into the Lago Sai Vai lake). Long abandoned, the fortress ruins were restored in 1976 and now form the basis of the *Pousada de São Tiago* hotel (see page 131), one of the most romantic places to stay in all Macau. Only the entranceway, foundations and eighteenth-century chapel survive from its

Museu Marítimo

Visiting Taipa Village and Coloane

For **Taipa Village**, take bus #11 from Avenida Almeida Ribeiro near Largo do Senado, bus #28A from the Jetfoil Terminal, or buses #22 or #33 from the *Lisboa* hotel; all these drop off near Taipa Stadium, a short walk from the village.

For **Coloane**, catch bus #21 or #21A from the *Lisboa* hotel; cutting straight across Taipa, these both travel down Coloane's west side to Coloane Village, from where the #21A and #26 continue via Cheoc Van beach to Hác Sá beach. From Taipa Village, take bus #15, which runs around Coloane's east side via the Westin Resort and Hác Sá beach, before terminating at Coloane Village.

original form, but – assuming you aren't too sloppily dressed – nobody will mind you entering the hotel to have a quick look at them.

Avenida da Amizade and the Porto Exterior

MAP P.110, POCKET MAP F12

The modern area southeast of Guia Hill is built on land reclaimed from the **Porto Exterior** (Outer Harbour) over the last few decades. The main artery here is the multi-laned **Avenida da Amizade**, whose southern end is marked by the orange-tiled **Lisboa**. It's Macau's most famous hotel and a roaring, 1930s-style casino, crowned by a multistorey circular drum done up like a wedding cake – though now completely outclassed by the adjacent, multicoloured **Grand Lisboa**, owned by the same management. Nearby on Avenida da Praia Grande, the **São Francisco barracks**, built in 1864 and painted a deep pink (as are all of Macau's military buildings), is the area's sole antique.

The whole Avenida da Amizade area is awash with casinos, and a **casino crawl** will provide a wide scope for people-watching, even if you're not interested in gambling. The **Casino Jai Alai** on Avenida do Dr Rodrigo Rodrigues is dark and verging on sleazy, with the feel of a hardcore den; the gold-windowed **Sands** on Avenida da Amizade has a Las Vegas slickness and colossal

open interior; the **Wynn** offers a sophisticated atmosphere; while the **Starworld** – despite a smart exterior and bright lighting – is another low-end deal specializing in tacky carpets and an ocean of slot machines.

Macau Cultural Centre houses the five-storey **Museum of Art** (Tues–Sun 10am–7pm; free. Currently closed for renovation and expansion works until mid-2019), whose collection of period paintings of Macau shares space with travelling exhibitions and temporary shows from overseas. The adjacent waterfront is dominated by a 20m bronze sculpture of Kun Iam.

Across Avenida da Amizade from the Sands casino, holidaying mainlanders pose in front of a **Golden Lotus Flower** sculpture, which sits beside the **Tourist Activity Centre**. The Centre's best feature is the **Museu do Vinho** (Wine Museum; 10am–6pm, closed Tues; free), dedicated to the history of Portuguese viniculture; entry gets you a free wine sample, and the shop sells some interesting vintages. Back over Avenida da Amizade between the Sands and the Jetfoil Terminal, **Fisherman's Wharf** is a themed open-air shopping plaza and entertainment complex incorporating a Chinese fort, a 40m-high man-made volcano, a Roman amphitheatre, re-creations of Chinese and European streets,

Macanese food

Macanese food – Macau's indigenous cuisine – blends Cantonese, Portuguese and colonial influences in varying degrees. Some dishes are straight Portuguese, such as *caldo verde* (cabbage and potato soup), *bacalhau* (dried salted cod) or plain grilled sardines; colonial dishes include "African Chicken" (served in a peppery peanut sauce) and Brazilian *feijoada* stew; while many cooks cross-fertilize foreign influences with Cantonese ingredients, creating "Chinese" dishes which are unlike anything found elsewhere. On top of this, there's a liking for un-Chinese accompaniments such as freshly baked bread, strong coffee and wine and port, plus **desserts** – including *Pastéis de Nata*, the ubiquitous baked custard tartlets.

and the usual restaurants and nightclubs. It's all rather lacklustre, with the air of a half-completed project that nobody really knows what to do with, though things perk up for specific events like the Grand Prix or Chinese New Year. From here, it's just a short walk on to the **Jetfoil Terminal**, outside of which you'll find a bus terminal (buses #3, #3A and #10A go to the *Lisboa* hotel or Largo do Senado).

Taipa Village

MAP P.110, POCKET MAP G12

Taipa's main point of interest is old **Taipa Village**, a few narrow streets surrounding a couple of

The Venetian casino

faded old squares. The Portuguese and Macanese **restaurants** here are one attraction, and on Sundays (noon–9pm) the streets are packed with a handicraft market. **Rua do Cunha** is the main street, a narrow pedestrianized lane lined with restaurants, *pasterlarias* and shops selling daily necessities. This exits into little **Feira da Carmo** square, surrounded by old pastel-coloured homes, at whose centre is the colonnaded nineteenth-century marketplace. Two nearby **temples** to Tin Hau and Pak Tai are similarly low-key, though Pak Tai's sports an impressive stone frieze above the entrance.

Exit Feira da Carmo square onto Rua Correia da Silva, and you'll soon see a flowing set of stairs lined with fig trees, which ascend to the small **Igreja do Carmo** (Lady of Carmel Church; Mon & Wed–Sun 8am–5pm; free). Just below sit five early twentieth-century mansions set up as Casa Museu (House Museum; Tues–Sun 10am–7pm; free). The first is comfortably airy and filled with tasteful period wooden furniture; others display old photos of Taipa and Coloane, costumed mannequins and temporary art shows.

Cotai and the Venetian

MAP P.110, POCKET MAP G13

The recently created land connecting Taipa with Coloane is

Pastéis de Nata

known as **Cotai**, an up-and-coming entertainment district featuring yet more casinos, including the **Venetian**, a full-scale reproduction of Venice's St Mark's Square. This houses the world's largest casino resort, with 850 gaming tables, 4100 slot machines and its own permanent **Cirque de Soleil** troupe, the first of many similar planned projects set to be developed in the near future. Further reclamation means that Cotai's western side now bumps up against the Chinese mainland, with the **Cotai Frontier Post** (not yet open to pedestrians) making access easy for coachloads of holidaying mainlanders.

Coloane

MAP P.110, POCKET MAP G13

Coloane was once a base for pirates who hid out in its cliffs and caves, seizing the cargoes of trading ships passing between Macau and China. Today, the island's main draws are its peaceful surroundings, beaches and a village with the usual mix of temples and colonial leftovers. **Parque de Seac Pai Van** (daily 8am–6pm; free) is a landscaped hillside with gardens, ponds, pavilions and paths up to a

20m-high white-marble statue of A-Ma which looks out over the water. **Coloane Village**, a cluster of cobbled lanes around a little central square and a seafront row of crumbling Chinese houses, shrines and temples, is also home to the pale yellow **St Francis Xavier chapel** (dawn to dusk; free), named after the sixteenth-century missionary who passed through Macau on his way to China and Japan. Out front is a monument with embedded cannons commemorating the repelling of the last pirate attack in 1910. Further along the waterfront, the **Tam Kung Temple** (daily 8.30am–5.30pm; free) houses a whalebone shaped into a Dragon Boat with oarsmen.

Coloane's southern coast has some good **beaches**, though the polluted water is unfit for swimming. **Cheoc Van** is well developed, featuring cafés and a swimming pool (Mon–Sat 8am–9pm, Sun 8am–midnight; MOP$10). **Hác Sá** is better, a long stretch of grey-black sand backed by pine trees, with plenty of picnic places, a beach bar and a recreation complex with another pool (Mon–Sat 8am–9pm, Sun 8am–midnight; MOP$15).

Restaurants

360° Café

MAP P.110, POCKET MAP E13
Level 60, Macau Tower ☎ 8988
8623, ⓦ macautower.com.mo. Daily
11.30am–10pm.

Smart revolving restaurant with
unparalleled city views, serving
Indian, Macanese and plain grilled
seafood. One way not to bankrupt
yourself is to opt for the set buffets
(from MOP$278).

A Lorcha

MAP P.110, POCKET MAP E12
Rua do Almirante Sérgio 298 ☎ 2831 3193,
ⓦ alorcha.com. Wed–Sun 12.30–3.00pm &
6.30–11.00pm.

This wood-beamed restaurant serves
outstanding Portuguese food and
is always busy. There's a large menu
of staples, including *serradura*,
a spectacular cream and biscuit
dessert. Around MOP$300 a head.

A Petisqueira

MAP P.110, POCKET MAP F13
15 Rua de S. João, Taipa Village ☎ 2882
5354. Tues–Fri 12.30–2.15pm & 6.45–10pm,
Sat & Sun 12.30–2.30pm and 6.45–10pm.

With its relaxing green interior,
this friendly, well-regarded
Portuguese restaurant has all the
usual favourites including delicious
home-style paella (MOP$158).

Clams at A Lorcha

Boa Mesa

MAP P.110, POCKET MAP E12
Travessa do S. Domingos 16A, between
the Sé and Largo do Senado ☎ 2838 9453.
Daily noon–10pm.

A relaxed, friendly place taking
pride in its farm-bred pig dishes and
sumptuous chocolate mousse. Set
meals start around MOP$110, and
even a la carte it's not too expensive.

Café Nga Tim/Chan Chi Mei

MAP P.110, POCKET MAP F13
Largo Eduardo Marques, in front of the
Xavier Chapel, Coloane Village ☎ 2888
2086. Daily noon–1am.

Inexpensive menu of Chinese,
Macanese and Portuguese dishes,
excelling in fresh seafood. Around
MOP$130 a head.

Café Ou Mun

MAP P.110, POCKET MAP E12
Travessa de Sâo Domingos 12 ☎ 2837
2207. Mon 11am–7pm, Tues–Sun
9am–10pm.

Café-restaurant with excellent
coffee, croissants and toasted
sandwiches; also serves light meals
at lunchtime.

Clube Militar

MAP P.110, POCKET MAP E12
Av. da Praia Grande 975 ☎ 2871 4010.
Mon–Fri 1.45–3.15pm & 7–11pm, Sat &
Sun noon–2.30pm & 7–11.pm.

This private club in the São
Francisco barracks has an elegant
colonial dining room open to the
public. The a la carte Portuguese
menu is dear, but the set-price
lunch buffet is fantastic value
(around MOP$150 a head). There's
also a 'no sportswear' dress code.

Fat Siu Lau

MAP P.110, POCKET MAP E11
Rua da Felicidade 64 ☎ 9857 3580,
ⓦ fatsiulau.com.mo. Daily noon–11pm.

One of Macau's oldest and most
famous Chinese restaurants.
Pigeon is the house speciality, but
otherwise their African chicken
(MOP$180) is also good.

Fernando

MAP P.110, POCKET MAP G13
Hác Sá Beach, Coloane ☏ 2888 2264. Daily noon–9.30pm; closed May 1.
The good Portuguese food and a casual, beach-side atmosphere make this long-running place a favourite with expats. Book in advance and be prepared to catch a taxi home. About MOP$200 per head.

Galo

MAP P.110, POCKET MAP F13
Calçado do Tronco Velho 10 ☏ 2882 7318, ⓦ galomacau.com. Daily noon–10.30pm.
Decorated in Portuguese country chic, with a menu sporting boiled meats, steaks, grilled squid or crab, and large mixed salads. Not fine cuisine, but hearty and full of flavour. Around $150 a head.

Litoral

MAP P.110, POCKET MAP E12
Rua do Almirante Sérgio 261 ☏ 2896 7878. Daily noon–3pm and 6–10.30pm.
Rated by some as serving the best Portuguese and Macanese food in Macau, with a menu based on old family recipes including curried crab and stewed pork with shrimp paste. Expect to pay $250 a head.

Lord Stow's Bakery

MAP P.110, POCKET MAP F13
Coloane Village Square, Coloane. Daily 7am–10pm.
Although British-owned, this is one of the best places to eat *natas* (baked custard tarts), made from a secret improved recipe without animal fat. Buy takeaways from the bakery, or have coffee and a light meal at their café around the corner.

Mariazinha

MAP P.110, POCKET MAP E11
Rua do Monte 8 ☏ 2835 7558. Mon–Sat 11.30am–3pm & 6.30–10pm.
Excellent Portuguese restaurant, offering everything from a roast pork sandwich (MOP$75) to a three-course blow-out of Iberian ham, cod and almond cake (around

Portuguese sardines at Fernando

MOP$500). They know their wines, too.

Nam Ping

MAP P.110, POCKET MAP E12
Rua de Cinco de Outubro 85 ☏ 2892 2267. Daily 6.30am–6.30pm.
Old-time Macanese café, serving home-baked sugared doughnuts, custard tarts, and ham and egg sandwiches. Nothing over MOP$25.

O Santos

MAP P.110, POCKET MAP F13
Rua da Cunha, Taipa Village ☏ 2822 7508. Wed–Sun noon–3pm & 6.30–10.30pm.
Hearty, home-style Portuguese food, delivered with little ceremony but in healthy portions: seafood, pork and bean stew, rabbit and roast suckling pig. Mains from MOP$120.

Riquexo

MAP P.00, POCKET MAP F11
Av. de Sidónio Pais 69-B ☏ 2856 5655. Mon–Fri 11am–6pm.
Basic Portuguese canteen, with little atmosphere and a limited menu but popular for its low prices. Go for the *feijoada* or curry chicken at MOP$28–55.

ACCOMMODATION

The Peninsula

Accommodation

Hong Kong has abundant accommodation, but space comes at a premium. The cheapest options downtown are at guesthouses in Tsim Sha Tsui and Mong Kok, offering beds in dormitories with shared bathrooms (around HK$150 per person), and doubles with en suites (around HK$450 per room). Hotels start at HK$1000 for a small room in the Kowloon backstreets, through to HK$2500 for a mid-range boutique place in a better location, and rise to over twice this for harbour views in Central or Tsim Sha Tsui. Options in the New Territories and islands include guesthouses, mid-range hotels and six remote, self-catering youth hostels (ⓦ yha.org.hk; beds from HK$115). Prices are highest during big sports events, Christmas and summer. Macau has budget options with doubles for under MOP$500, mid-range hotels for MOP$1200 and a luxury end catered to by casino resorts (over MOP$2000). Rates are higher on Friday and Saturday nights, and during the November Grand Prix. Prices given are for the cheapest double room unless specified; hostel prices are for a dorm bed per person. Hostel and guesthouse prices are inclusive; in hotels, a ten percent service fee – and in Macau a further five percent tax – is charged on top.

Central to Kennedy Town

GARDEN VIEW (YWCA) MAP.28, POCKET MAP D7. 1 Macdonnell Rd (green minibus #1A from City Hall) Central ⓦ Central ☎ 2877 3737, ⓦ yhk.com.hk. Small rooms, but well located near the Botanical Gardens and Lower Peak Tram Terminal. **$1500**

LAN KWAI FONG HOTEL MAP P.28, POCKET MAP C5. 3 Kau U Fong ⓦ Sheung Wan ☎ 3650 0000, ⓦ lankwaifonghotel. com.hk. This well-run boutique hotel has rooms decked out with antique-style Chinese furnishings and is located near old market streets along the Central–Sheung Wan border. **$1200**

MADERA HOLLYWOOD MAP P.28, POCKET MAP C6. 53 Hollywood Rd, Central ⓦ Central Exit D2 ☎ 3913 2888, ⓦ maderagroup.com. Bright colours disguise off-the-peg furnishings, but generously sized suites make this a good option close to Lan Kwai Fong. **$2000**

MANDARIN ORIENTAL MAP P.28, POCKET MAP E6. 5 Connaught Rd ⓦ Central ☎ 2522 0111, ⓦ mandarinoriental.com. Considered by many to be Hong Kong's best hotel, with excellent facilities and decor (antique-filled rooms with balconies, and corridors featuring eighteenth-century Chinese textiles), and an ideal location. **$4000**

MOUNT DAVIS YOUTH HOSTEL MAP P.28, POCKET MAP A6. Mount Davis ⓦ Kennedy Town ☎ 2817 5715, ⓦ yha.org. hk. Perched on a mountain above Kennedy Town, this self-catering hostel also has a campsite and superb harbour views. Get the free shuttle bus from Kennedy Town MTR, Exit C – check the website for times – or catch a taxi (around $40 plus $10 per item of luggage). Dorms **$165**, doubles **$440**

Booking accommodation

Book Hong Kong accommodation directly through hotel websites; for general hotel information visit ⓦ discoverhongkong.com/eng, which has extensive listings and contact details. For Macau, either book direct with accommodation or through a travel agent in Hong Kong.

Wan Chai

CONRAD MAP P.50, POCKET MAP F7. Pacific Place, 88 Queensway ⓜ Admiralty ☎ 2521 3838, ⓦ conradhotels3.hilton. com. Modern hotel with well-equipped rooms. Its position on the upper floors of the Pacific Place towers ensures views from all rooms. **$3800**

GRAND HYATT MAP P.50, POCKET MAP H6. 1 Harbour Rd ⓜ Wan Chai ☎ 2588 1234, ⓦ hongkong.grand.hyatt.com. Part of the Convention and Exhibition Centre complex, with harbour views and a luxurious feel. It also has the largest hotel swimming pool in Hong Kong. **$2600**

HOTEL INDIGO MAP P.50, POCKET MAP H8. 246 Queen's Road East ⓜ Wan Chai Exit A3 ☎ 800 877 8987 ⓦ ihg.com. Smart new place in an interesting corner of town, close to some quirky side-streets, a wide range of restaurants, and a couple of temples. Rooms are compact but modern and stylish, plus there's a rooftop pool and a cool-casual restaurant. **$1800**

KEW GREEN MAP P.50, POCKET MAP H7. 41–49 Hennessy Rd ⓜ Wan Chai ☎ 2861 1166, ⓦ kewgreenhotelwanchai.com. Modern, chic place, although the design and layout of the rooms is standard: bed, desk, bathroom, TV and exactly enough floor space to navigate between them. **$1200**

RENAISSANCE HARBOUR VIEW MAP P.50, POCKET MAP H6. 1 Harbour Rd ⓜ Wan Chai ☎ 2802 8888, ⓦ marriott.com. Splendid views and the same expense-account clientele as the adjacent *Grand Hyatt* – whose facilities you get to use – though generally lower rates. **$2500**

Causeway Bay

JETVAN TRAVELLER'S HOUSE MAP P.50, POCKET MAP L6. 4/F, 4A Fairview Mansions, 51 Paterson St ⓜ Causeway Bay ☎ 2890 8133, ⓦ jetvan.com. Popular guesthouse with eight rooms, all with telephone, a/c, TV and bathroom, though some are windowless. **$500**

PARK LANE MAP P.50, POCKET MAP L6. 310 Gloucester Rd ⓜ Causeway Bay ☎ 2293 8888, ⓦ parklane.com.hk. Smart option for business or upmarket travellers, overlooking Victoria Park; well placed for the MTR. **$2030**

WANG FAT MAP P.50, POCKET MAP L6. 3/F, Paterson Building, 47 Paterson St ⓜ Causeway Bay ☎ 2392 6868, ⓦ hostel. hk. Basic, bright and clean hostel with a free laundry service and multilingual manager. Dorms **$130**, doubles **$390**

YESINN MAP P.50, POCKET MAP K6. 2/F, Nan Yip Building, 472 Hennessy Rd ⓜ Causeway Bay Exit C ☎ 2231 4567 ⓦ yesinn.com. Friendly hostel with both mixed and single-sex dorms, plus en-suite doubles in a separate building. Rooms are cramped even for Hong Kong, but it's clean and the rooftop "garden" terrace is a plus. Dorms **$180**, doubles **$400**

Tsim Sha Tsui

1946 BOUTIQUE (精品旅館) MAP P.66, POCKET MAP B17. 8/F Majestic House, 80 Nathan Rd (in Cameron Rd) ⓜ Tsim Sha Tsui ☎ 9488 7788 ⓔ bennyleeck@ hotmail.com.hk. Clean, friendly and secure guesthouse; rooms vary in size from cramped to comfortable, though bathrooms unusually large for this kind of place. **$500**

BENITO MAP P.66, POCKET MAP B17. 7–7B Cameron Rd, Tsim Sha Tsui Ⓜ Tsim Sha Tsui ☎ 3653 0388, Ⓦ hotelbenito.com. Bright, clean boutique hotel close to all that matters in Tsim Sha Tsui. Cheaper rooms are small. **$800**

BP INTERNATIONAL HOUSE MAP P.66, POCKET MAP A16. 8 Austin Rd Ⓜ Jordan ☎ 2376 1111, Ⓦ bpih.com.hk. Run by the Scouting organization, this tidy, excellent-value place has smart doubles facing Kowloon Park, along with triples and quads. **$1000**

GARDEN HOSTEL MAP P.66, POCKET MAP B17. Block F4, 3/F, Mirador Mansions, 56–58 Nathan Rd Ⓜ Tsim Sha Tsui ☎ 2311 1183, Ⓦ gardenhostel.com.hk. Laidback hostel with a garden terrace. Eight-person dorms are male- or female-only, and rooms are sparklingly clean. Dorms **$120**, doubles **$350**

GERMANY HOSTEL MAP P.66, POCKET MAP B17. Block D, 6/F, Chungking Mansions, 36–44 Nathan Rd Ⓜ Tsim Sha Tsui ☎ 9832 4807, Ⓦ germanyhostelhk. com. Clean and friendly, though rooms are very small. Dorms **$160**, doubles **$330**

INTERCONTINENTAL MAP P.66, POCKET MAP B18. 18 Salisbury Rd Ⓜ Tsim Sha Tsui ☎ 2721 1211, Ⓦ intercontinental. com. Rival in quality to the *Peninsula* and the preferred hotel of many business tycoons. **$1900**

LEE GARDEN MAP P.66, POCKET MAP B17. Block A, 8/F, Fook Kiu Mansion, 34–36 Cameron Rd Ⓜ Tsim Sha Tsui ☎ 2367 2284, Ⓦ leegarden.com.hk. Secure, clean and comfortable range of budget singles, doubles and triples in a private apartment building; a bit expensive for what you get though. **$600**

LUXE MANOR MAP P.66, POCKET MAP B16. 39 Kimberley Rd, Tsim Sha Tsui Ⓜ Tsim Sha Tsui ☎ 3763 8888, Ⓦ theluxemanor.com. A boutique option, with stylish themed rooms to appeal or appal. Their *Aspasia* restaurant draws the chic and almost-famous to dine. **$1000**

MARCO POLO HONGKONG, MARCO POLO GATEWAY, MARCO POLO PRINCE MAP P.66, POCKET MAP A17–A18. Harbour City, Canton Rd Ⓜ Tsim Sha Tsui ☎ 2113 1888, Ⓦ marcopolohotels.com. The Harbour City complex houses three different hotels under the same *Marco Polo* umbrella. They're all fairly fancy, and guests can use any hotel's facilities. Only the *Hongkong* has harbour views; those at the *Prince* overlook Kowloon Park. **$1700**

PENINSULA MAP P.66, POCKET MAP B18. Salisbury Rd Ⓜ Tsim Sha Tsui ☎ 2920 2888, Ⓦ peninsula.com. Possibly the grandest hotel in Hong Kong, the *Peninsula* has been putting visitors up in unrivalled style since the late 1920s. Its elegant colonial wings have been overshadowed by the new central tower, which provides harbour views. **$3600**

SALISBURY YMCA MAP P.66, POCKET MAP B18. 41 Salisbury Rd Ⓜ Tsim Sha Tsui ☎ 2268 7888, Ⓦ ymcahk.org.hk. For the price, probably the best hotel in Hong Kong, especially compared to the adjacent *Peninsula*. The recently-renovated rooms are all good, but if possible, get one with a harbour view. Facilities include indoor pools and a fitness centre, with a generous buffet breakfast included. Doubles **$970**, harbour-view **$1510**

Jordan/Yau Ma Tei

BOOTH LODGE MAP P.78, POCKET MAP B13. 7/F, 11 Wing Sing Lane Ⓜ Jordan ☎ 2771 9266, Ⓦ salvationarmy.org.hk. A Salvation Army hotel close to the Jade and Temple Street markets. Rooms are functional, and there's a restaurant and café. **$1100**

KINGS MAP P.78, POCKET MAP A15. 50 Temple St, Yau Ma Tei Ⓜ Yau Ma Tei ☎ 3701 0888, Ⓦ kingshotelhk.com. This newly-renovated budget hotel sports clean, comfortable, simple rooms, plus it's close to the night market and some bustling street life – which means it can be noisy after dark. **$900**

NATHAN MAP P.78, POCKET MAP B14. 378 Nathan Rd Ⓜ Jordan ☎ 2388 5141, nathanhotel.com. Somewhat non-descript budget business venue, of the type springing up all over the world; but it's tidy, good-value, close to Jordan MTR, and they throw in a decent buffet breakfast. Helpful staff too. **$1000**

SILKA SEAVIEW HOTEL MAP P.78, POCKET MAP A14. 268 Shanghai St ⓦ Yau Ma Tei ☏ 2782 0882, ⓦ silkahotel.com/seaview. No sea view, but rooms are bright, modern and cheerful, and you're close to the night market, temple and jade market. Advance bookings get serious discounts. **$950**

Mong Kok

DRAGON HOSTEL MAP P.78, POCKET MAP A11. Room 707, 7/F, Sincere House, 83 Argyle St ⓜ Mong Kok ☏ 2395 0577, ⓦ dragonhostel.com. Guesthouse with helpful management and comparatively large single, double and family rooms that represent a good deal compared with what you'd get in Tsim Sha Tsui. Long-stay rates available. **$400**

ROYAL PLAZA MAP P.78, POCKET MAP B10. 193 Prince Edward Rd West ⓜ Mong Kok ☏ 2928 8822, ⓦ royalplaza.com.hk. This smart hotel sits on top of Mong Kok MTR station, with an entrance in the Grand Century Place shopping plaza. The 469 rooms come with all the usual amenities but are fairly characterless. There's also a 40m swimming pool, gym, an enormous ballroom and a library. **$1500**

Sham Shui Po

MEI HO HOUSE YOUTH HOSTEL MAP P.78, POCKET MAP A10. Block 41, 70 Berwick St ⓜ Sham Shui Po ☏ 3728 3500, ⓦ yha.org.hk. Set in a historic housing estate, this is the most usefully located YHA in Hong Kong, so it's pricey and often booked out. Institutional but clean dorms and doubles, plus a good café/restaurant (open to the general public too). Dorms **$300**, doubles **$800**

The New Territories

BRADBURY JOCKEY CLUB YOUTH HOSTEL MAP P.88. 66 Tai Mei Tuk Rd, Tai Mei Tuk, Tai Po. Bus #75K from ⓜ Tai Po Market ☏ 2662 5123, ⓦ yha.org.hk. From the bus terminus, walk towards Plover Cove Reservoir and the hostel is a few minutes ahead on the left. It has two- to eight-bed rooms plus 94 dorm beds, sited at the edge of Plover Cove Country Park. Self-catering facilities only, so bring supplies. Dorms **$100**, 4-bed rooms **$600**

REGAL RIVERSIDE MAP P.88. Tai Chung Kiu Rd, Sha Tin ⓜ Sha Tin Wai ☏ 2649 7878, ⓦ regalhotel.com. A comfortable, rather isolated conference-style hotel, about a 15min walk from central Sha Tin. The large rooms are a steal compared to what you'd pay in Tsim Sha Tsui or Central. **$850**

SZE LOK YUEN YOUTH HOSTEL MAP P.88. Tai Mo Shan, Tsuen Wan. Bus #51 from ⓜ Tsuen Wan, then a 40min walk. ☏ 2488 8188, ⓦ yha.org.hk. This place has camping facilities and 92 dorm beds at the start of trails up Tai Mo Shan's peak (see page 87); self-catering only, so bring supplies. Dorms **$115**

Lantau

NGONG PING S.G. DAVIS YOUTH HOSTEL MAP P.100. Ngong Ping. 500m from Po Lin Monastery, signed along the Lantau Trail (see page 99) ☏ 2985 5610, ⓦ yha.org.hk. Camping facilities and 46 beds are available at this basic, self-catering hostel. Dorms **$135**, doubles **$376**

NOVOTEL CITYGATE MAP P.100. 51 Man Tung Rd, Tung Chung ⓜ Tung Chung ☏ 3602 8888, ⓦ novotel.com. Right next to the Tung Chung MTR and Ngong Ping 360, and close to the airport. Rates are a bargain compared to the downtown areas, and the website often advertises inexpensive last-minute deals. **$1300**

SILVERMINE BEACH RESORT MAP P.100. Mui Wo ☏ 6810 0111, ⓦ silvermineresort.com. Overlooking the beach at Silvermine Bay, this is comfortable and great value for money. There's a swimming pool, gym, sauna, tennis courts and all the usual business paraphernalia. **$1200**

Lamma and Cheung Chau

B&B MAP P.105. Chung Wan beach ☏ 2986 9990, ⓦ ibnb.com.hk. The original of this local chain offers bed-and-breakfast with a roof terrace for views over the town and sea. **$650**

BALI HOLIDAY RESORT MAP P.105. 8 Main St, Yung Shue Wan ☏ 2982 4504, ⓦ lammabali.com. Apartment block with spacious rooms, with or without views and kitchenettes – more modern than *Sunrise*, but further back from the water. **$350**

BELLA VISTA MIAMI RESORT MAP P.105. East Bay ☏ 2981 7299, ⓦ miamicheungchau.com.hk. A huge variety of rooms in a residential block near the east beach. The better options are worth the extra cost. **$550**

CONCERTO INN MAP P.105. 28 Hung Shing Ye Beach, Yung Shue Wan ☏ 2982 1668, ⓦ concertoinn.com.hk. Lamma's best hotel, offering rooms with balconies overlooking the beach, satellite TV, videos and fridges – some have kitchens. **$920**

KATHMANDU GUESTHOUSE MAP P.105. Above Bubbles Laundry in Yung Shue Wan ☏ 2982 0028. This no-frills place has been going forever and offers dorm beds as well as doubles at some of the lowest rates on the island. Dorms **$120**

SUNRISE HOLIDAY RESORT MAP P.105. Yung Shue Wan ☏ 2982 0606, ⓦ ammaresort.com. Close to the ferry, with a range of bright, simple self-contained flats, some with sea views. **$550**

WARWICK MAP P.105. East Bay ☏ 2981 0081, ⓦ warwickhotel.com.hk. Overlooking Tung Wan beach, rooms at this concrete box of a hotel have balconies, private baths and cable TV. There's also a terrace café and pool. **$750**

Eastern Macau

LISBOA MAP P.110. Av. de Lisboa 2–4 ☏ 2888 3888, ⓦ hotelisboa.com. A monstrous orange building with around a thousand rooms, a bundle of 24hr casinos on several floors, shops, bars and restaurants, and an outdoor pool and sauna. MOP$1000, royal tower rooms MOP$1200

MANDARIN ORIENTAL MAP P.110. POCKET MAP F12. Av. da Amizade ☏ 8805 8888, ⓦ mandarinoriental.com/macau. Excellent service and facilities at this upmarket resort, tailor-made for families (children's club and poolside restaurant), corporate groups (a team-building climbing wall and trapeze) and the more traditional Macau visitor (casino and popular bar). MOP$1900

METROPOLE MAP P.110. Av. da Praia Grande 493–501 ☏ 2838 8166, ⓦ macauctshotel.com. This well-placed central hotel is just back from the Praia Grande, and good value if you're looking for standard rooms with all the trimmings at a good price. MOP$1000

NEW NAM PAN MAP P.110. Av. de D. João IV 8 ☏ 2848 2842. Central, friendly, modern guesthouse with nine smallish rooms. Furnishings are a bit plain, and the beds are hard, but it's clean and good value for money. MOP$580

ROYAL MAP P.110. Estrada da Vitoria 2–4 ☏ 2855 2222, ⓦ hotelroyal.com.mo. An ageing but good-value high-rise, close to the Fortaleza da Guia. A 10min walk from Largo do Senado, and well equipped, with standard and deluxe doubles, suites and a pool. MOP$1300

SANDS MAP P.110. Largo do Monte Carlo 23, Av. da Amizade ☏ 2888 3388, ⓦ sandsmacao.com. The city's first foreign-owned casino offers a choice of luxury suites overlooking the city or bay. MOP$1200

WYNN MAP P.110, POCKET MAP F12. Rua Cidade da Sintra ☏ 8986 9966, ⓦ wynnmacau.com. Macau's most stylish upmarket casino-resort, balancing opulence with taste. MOP$2100

Central and southern Macau

KO WAH (KOU VA) MAP P.110. 3/F, Rua Felicidade 71 ☎ 2893 0755/2837 5599. Clean and basic hotel accessed by lift from the cupboard-sized street lobby. Some rooms are brighter and better than others. MOP$500

MAN VA MAP P.110. Rua da Felicidade ☎ 2838 8655, Ⓦ manvahotelmacau. com. On a street lined with red wooden doors, this simple hotel has clean, modern rooms; bathrooms are spacious and the management helpful, though they don't speak English. Excellent value for money. MOP$450

OLE LONDON MAP P.110. Praça Ponte e Horta 4–6 ☎ 2893 7761, Ⓦ olelondonhotel.com. Smart boutique hotel with plain, modern rooms. The cheapest options are windowless, so it's best to pay a bit extra to get one overlooking the square. MOP$750

PENSÃO WA FAT MAP P.110. Av. da Praia Grande 622 ☎ 2871 6415. Clean, bright budget hotel; rooms are tiny but have bathrooms. MOP$900

POUSADA DE SÃO TIAGO MAP P.110, POCKET MAP E12. Av da República ☎ 2837 8111, Ⓦ saotiago.com.mo. Upmarket hotel inside the shell of a seventeenth-century fortress, temporarily shut during construction of Macau's light rail system. MOP$2888, balconied rooms with views around MOP$500 extra

SANVA MAP P.110. Rua da Felicidade 65–67 Ⓦ sanvahotel.com. Best budget deal in town, with spotless rooms in an early 1900s building featuring wooden shutters and balconies over Rua Felicidade. MOP$260

SUN SUN MAP P.110. Praça Ponte e Horta 14–16 ☎ 2893 9393, Ⓦ bestwestern.com. Smart hotel where the upper floors have a view of the inner harbour. Rooms have TV and bath, and there's plenty of marble and wood in the lobby. MOP$800

TOWNS WELL MAP P.110. Calçada das Verdades 6 ☎ 2835 6868. This well-located budget hotel's cylindrical, pink-tiled exterior has clean and reasonably spacious rooms and come equipped with everything you'll need. The only downside is a faint smell of cigarettes in some rooms. MOP$650

Coloane

GRANDE COLOANE RESORT MAP P.110, POCKET MAP G13. Estrada de Hác Sá ☎ 2887 1111, Ⓦ grandcoloane.com. Set on Hác Sá's narrow beach, with terraced rooms spread across the hillside. The hotel offers Macau's only 18-hole golf course, two pools and a jacuzzi, with modern, spacious rooms. MOP$1100

POUSADA DE COLOANE MAP P.110, POCKET MAP G13. Praia de Cheoc Van ☎ 2888 2143, Ⓦ hotelpcoloane.com.mo. A quirky hotel with 22 rooms, each with its own terrace overlooking the beach. Rooms on the top floor are huge, with sofas, tables and king-sized beds. Apart from its own Portuguese restaurant and a stretch of sand, there's not much else here. MOP$650

VENETIAN MAP P.110, POCKET MAP G13. Cotai ☎ 2882 8877, Ⓦ venetianmacao. com. An incredible full-scale replica of St Mark's Square in Venice (including canals with gondolas) fronts a three thousand-room resort, convention centre and casino complex: the convention space here alone is greater than that available in Hong Kong. A sign of the wealth accruing in Macau. From MOP$1200

ESSENTIALS

Dragon Boat Festival

Arrival

All arrival points in Hong Kong and Macau – airports, train and bus stations, ferry ports and border crossings – are either centrally located or efficiently connected to the downtown areas by public transport.

By air

Hong Kong International Airport (⊕ hongkongairport.com) is located at Chek Lap Kok, 34km west of Hong Kong Island and just off Lantau Island. The **Airport Express train** (every eight minutes; 6am–12.45am) runs via Kowloon (20min; $90) and Central Airport Express stations on Hong Kong Island (24min; HK$100). Buy **tickets** from machines or service desks in the arrival halls; the desk offers discounts for same-day returns or people travelling together. It's still some way from Kowloon and Central stations to accommodation, so make use of **free shuttle buses** (around 6am–11pm; 2–3 an hour) to various hotels; you don't have to be a guest to use the service.

Airport buses (6am–midnight, plus skeleton night service) can take over an hour to get from the airport into town. Buy tickets at customer service desks or on the bus (drivers do not give change). Useful services include the #A11 to Causeway Bay via Central and Wan Chai (every 15–25min; HK$40), and the #A21 to Mong Kok, Yau Ma Tei and Tsim Sha Tsui (every 10min; HK$33).

Taxis from the airport cost HK$300–400 into town, and there may be extra charges for luggage ($5 per piece) and for tunnel tolls to Hong Kong Island ($10–15 depending on the tunnel; drivers can legally request you pay the return toll too).

Macau International Airport (⊕ macau-airport.com/en) is located at the eastern side of Taipa Island, from where **airport bus** #AP1 (20min; MOP$4.20) meets all flights and runs to the Jetfoil Terminal and Lisboa hotel on Avenida da Amizade; a **taxi** into town costs about MOP$40. A light rail line into town is also currently under construction.

Helicopters (HK$/MOP$4300 each way; ⊕ skyshuttlehk.com) also shuttle between Hong Kong's Macau Ferry Terminal in Sheung Wan and Macau's Jetfoil Terminal on Avenida da Amizade; see "By ferry" for public transport available at either terminus.

By ferry

Hong Kong has two downtown ferry ports: the **Hong Kong–Macau Ferry Terminal** in the Shun Tak Centre in Sheung Wan, Hong Kong Island (on top of Sheung Wan MTR station), which handles traffic to Macau and Shenzhen airport in China; and the **China Ferry Terminal** on Canton Road, Tsim Sha Tsui, Kowloon (from where Tsim Sha Tsui MTR station is a 10–15min walk), whose services include Macau and various Chinese towns through the Pearl River delta.

Macau also has two ports: the central **Outer Harbour Jetfoil Terminal** on Avenida da Amizade for Shekou (Shenzhen Port) and Hong Kong ferries (connected to town by buses #3, #3A, #10, #28A, #28B and #32 via the Lisboa hotel; and the #10 or #10A via Largo do Senado); and the new **Taipa Terminal**, next to Macau airport, which besides Hong Kong also handles traffic to Shenzhen airport.

All regular passenger ferries between Hong Kong, Macau and Shenzhen are run by **Turbojet** (⊕ turbojet.com.hk), which operate about 7am to midnight depending on the route, and cost from $171 between Hong Kong and Macau (1hr), $235 between Hong Kong and Shenzhen airport (1hr), $245 between Macau and Shenzhen airport (1hr), and $238 between Macau and Shekou (1hr). Ferry tickets can be bought on the day, though for Macau it's advisable to book in advance on Friday, Saturday and Sunday.

By train
Direct trains to Hong Kong from Guangzhou, Shanghai and Beijing in China arrive at Hung Hom Railway Station in Tsim Sha Tsui East (ⓦmtr.com.hk). You'll also end up here if you cross the border on foot from Shenzhen to Lo Wu or Lok Ma Chau, then catch the East Rail Line (see "Getting around") down through the New Territories. At Hung Hom, there are taxis and buses, or catch the MTR one stop south to its terminus at Tsim Sha Tsui East station, which exits into Middle Road. There are no trains to Macau, though you can catch one from elsewhere in China to the border town of Zhuhai and then cross over on foot.

By bus
There are buses to downtown Hong Kong from the Chinese border crossings and Shenzhen airport (about 30km north); most of these terminate at company depots in Wan Chai, and a few run to Mong Kok in Kowloon. You can book through CTS Hong Kong ⓦctshk.com/english.

On foot
Hong Kong has several pedestrian border crossings between Shenzhen in China and the New Territories, but by far the most popular is at Lo Wu (6am–midnight). Formalities are straightforward, and you end up at Lo Wu MTR station, from where trains run south via Tai Po, Sha Tin and Mong Kok to Hung Hom rail station in Kowloon in forty minutes (see "By train" for onward connections). In Macau, walk across the border via the customs complex (7am–midnight) and catch taxis or buses to your destination; buses #10 and #3 run down Avenida de Almeida Ribeiro to the centre.

Getting around

Hong Kong has an excellent integrated public transport system. Underground and overground trains, trams, buses and ferries connect almost every part of the territory, and are cheap and simple to use. Macau's public transport comprises buses and taxis, with a light rail system under construction. Hong Kong tour operators also offer easy ways of day-tripping to Macau and seeing the highlights.

The MTR (Mass Transit Railway)
Hong Kong's speedy **MTR** (daily 6am–1am; trains every few min; ⓦmtr.com.hk) comprises a handful of lines connecting Hong Kong Island with Kowloon, along with the Lantau line, Airport Express Line (AEL), and East Rail and West Rail lines into the New Territories. Maps are colour-coded and bilingual, and **tickets** cost between HK$4.50 and HK$52 one-way. Ticket machines are on the station concourse – some don't give change and some only take coins. The MTR gets extremely crowded during **rush hour** (8–9.30am & 5.30–7pm).

Light Rail (LR)
Hong Kong's **Light Rail** (ⓦmtr.com.hk) is an electric, tram-like network linking the western New Territory towns. The only time visitors are likely to use it is to reach the Hong Kong Wetland Park at Tin Shui Wai. Fares cost HK$5–7 per journey.

Buses

Hong Kong buses (daily 6am–midnight; skeleton night bus service after midnight; ⓦnwstbus.com.hk) cover just about every corner of the region. Each bus is numbered and marked with the destination in English and Chinese, along with a letter: "M" means that it links with an MTR station; "R" buses only run on Sundays and public holidays; "X" buses are express services with limited stops; and "N" buses are night services. You need the exact fare (HK$3–48 per trip) or an Octopus card; no change is given.

Minibuses – the vehicles are banded in green or red – parallel downtown bus routes and also run out to remoter places, but you might need local knowledge to find the right one, as they're mostly signed only in Chinese; you pay the same way.

Macau's buses (daily 7am–11pm; ⓦdsat.gov.mo) operate on circular routes. Fares are MOP$3.20 for city routes, MOP$4.20 for Taipa and the airport, and MOP$5 for Coloane ($6.40 to Hác Sá). Pay the driver the exact fare as you get on.

Trams

Double-decker **trams** (daily 6am–midnight; ⓦhktramways.com) rattle along the north shore of Hong Kong Island between Kennedy Town and Causeway Bay; some detour around Happy Valley Racecourse. You alight at the back and pay the flat HK$2.30 **fare** as you exit from the front. Destinations are marked on the front in English.

Ferries

Hong Kong's famous **Star Ferry** (ⓦstarferry.com.hk) crosses the harbour from Tsim Sha Tsui to either Central Ferry Piers or to Wan Chai, just east of the Convention and Exhibition Centre. The low, beamy, old-fashioned vessels are painted a distinctive green and named Morning Star, Evening Star etc; decks are wooden and you sit on reversible benches. Services run every few minutes daily (6/7am until 7–11pm, depending on the route), unless suspended by bad weather.

Inter-island ferries leave from the Outlying Islands Ferry Piers in front of the IFC2 tower in Central – see island accounts on see pages 27, 100 and 105 for details. For Hong Kong–Macau ferries, see "Arrival" on page 134.

Taxis

Hong Kong's taxis are relatively cheap: HK$24 for the first 2km, then HK$1.70 per 200m, though there might be surcharges for carrying luggage and using the cross-harbour tunnels. Taxis are colour-coded for region: red on Hong Kong Island and in Kowloon; green in the New Territories; and blue on Lantau. Taxis for hire display a red flag in the windscreen and an illuminated "Taxi" sign on the roof. Make sure the driver turns the meter on when you get in (though rip-offs

Octopus Cards

For heavy public transport use in Hong Kong, buy an **Octopus Card** (ⓦoctopus.com.hk/en), a rechargeable ticket available from train ticket offices for travel on the MTR, the Airport Express, Light Rail, trams, most buses, most ferries and minibuses. The card costs an initial HK$150, comprising HK$100 usable value and HK$50 deposit. To top up, add credit at machines in rail stations or over the counter at any 7-Eleven store. To use, scan them over sensors at the ticket gates or on board vehicles.

are rare). Don't expect drivers to speak English, apart from the names of hotels and streets. If you get stuck, gesture to the driver to radio his control centre, and ask them to translate.

Macau's taxis are also inexpensive: MOP$19 for the first 1.6km, then MOP$2 for every 230m, plus MOP$3 for each piece of luggage. There's also a MOP$2 surcharge between Taipa and Coloane, and a MOP$5 surcharge for airport pick-ups.

Tours

Operators running **English-language tours** in Hong Kong include the Hong Kong Tourist Board (ⓦ discoverhongkong.com), Splendid Tours (ⓦ splendid.hk) and Gray Line Tours (ⓦ grayline.com.hk). Between them, they arrange half- or full-day coach tours of Hong Kong Island and Kowloon (including sites such as Man Mo Temple, The Peak, Temple Street Night Market, Aberdeen harbour and Stanley Market) from HK$560; a half-day run around Lantau's main sights (HK$850); and ever-popular horseracing tours, which get you into the swanky members' enclosure for a buffet dinner and some racing tips (race days only, dress and minimum age rules apply; from HK$1280 depending on the event). Sunset harbour cruises with a seafood meal are HK$620, and they also offer a full-day tour to Macau (HK$1120).

For a harbour cruise, try Aqualuna (ⓦ aqualuna.com.hk), Hong Kong's last traditional junk – though with cut-down sails. A 45min evening jaunt plus a sundowner costs HK$220, or try the cruise to Stanley (HK$280 one-way, or HK$400 return).

For an evening sampling local street food, try Urban Discovery (ⓦ hongkongfoodietours.com) or Big Foot (ⓦ bigfoottour.com).com. Big Foot and Hong Kong Less Travelled (ⓦ itishk.com) also offer walking tours all over Hong Kong.

Directory A–Z

Addresses

Addresses in Hong Kong are easy to read but there is occasional confusion with street level, which is "Ground Floor" (here written G/F) in English, but "First Floor" (1/F) in Chinese. In Macau, lengthy street names are often abbreviated, so that "Avenida do Infante Dom Henrique" becomes "Av do Infante D Henrique".

Cinema

Once hosting the world's third-largest film industry – no mean achievement for a place with just seven million inhabitants – Hong Kong's output has long-since been overtaken by mainland China, even as cinema itself has been undermined by online media.

Locally made products include police thrillers, kung fu epics, romances and comedies. Cinemas in Hong Kong are mostly multi-screen complexes run by MCL (ⓦ mclcinema. com), UA (ⓦ uacinemas.com.hk) and Golden Harvest (ⓦ goldenharvest. com), and show a mix of international blockbusters (usually screened in the original language, with Chinese subtitles) alongside Chinese-language releases from China, Hong Kong and Taiwan.

Crime

Despite recent politically-motivated demonstrations, Hong Kong and Macau are orderly, relatively safe places for visitors. The usual precautions apply: lock valuables inside bags in hotel

Emergency numbers

☎ 999 for fire, police or ambulance from a Hong Kong or Macau landline; ☎ 112 from a mobile.

rooms, watch out for pickpockets in crowds, and don't wander the backstreets at night. Hong Kong's Police Headquarters are at Arsenal Street, Wan Chai (☎ 3661 1602); Macau's are at Praçeta de 1 de Outubro (☎ 2857 3333).

Electricity

Mains power in Hong Kong and Macau is 220–240V. Hong Kong uses plugs with three square pins (as in the UK); Macau uses both these and plugs with two round pins (as in Europe, China and the US). You can buy adaptors at street markets, shops on the ground floor of Chungking Mansions, or many other places for HK$5–10.

Embassies and consulates

Australia, 23/F, Harbour Centre, 25 Harbour Rd, Wan Chai ☎ 2827 8881; Canada, Berkshire House, 25 Westlands Rd, Quarry Bay ☎ 3719 4700; **China**, 7/F, Lower Block, China Resources Building, 26 Harbour Rd, Wan Chai ☎ 3413 2424; **India**, 16/F, United Centre, 95 Queensway, Admiralty ☎ 3970 9900; **Ireland**, 20/F, 33 De Voeux Rd, Central ☎ 2535 0700; **Japan**, 46/F, One Exchange Square, Central ☎ 2522 1184; **Korea**, 5/F, Far East Finance Centre, 16 Harcourt Rd, Central ☎ 2529 4141; **Malaysia**, 24/F, Malaysia Building, 47–50 Gloucester Rd, Wan Chai ☎ 2821 0800; **New Zealand**, 6501 Central Plaza, 18 Harbour Rd, Wan Chai ☎ 2525 5044; **Philippines**, 14/F, United Centre, 95 Queensway, Admiralty ☎ 2823 8501; **Singapore**, 901–2 Tower 1, Admiralty Centre, Admiralty ☎ 2527 2212; **South Africa**, 19/F, Central Plaza, 18 Harbour Rd, Wan Chai ☎ 3926 4300; **Thailand**, 8/F, Fairmont House, 8 Cotton Tree Drive, Central ☎ 2521 6481; **UK**, 1 Supreme Court Rd, Admiralty ☎ 2901 3000; US, 26 Garden Rd, Central ☎ 2523 9011; **Vietnam**, 15/F, Great Smart Tower, 230 Wan Chai Rd, Wan Chai ☎ 2591 4510.

LGBTQ travellers

Macau has no LGBTQ scene at all, and Hong Kong's is low-key considering the number of people here. *Dimsum* (☻ dimsum-hk.com) is Hong Kong's gay lifestyle magazine, heavy on articles, lighter on listings and reviews; these are better covered in the "Queer HK" section of *Time Out Hong Kong* (☻ timeout.com.hk).

Health

GPs in Hong Kong charge around $570 a consultation; ask at your accommodation for the closest one. Hong Kong's government hospitals charge $1230 for an Accident & Emergency visit, or $5100 a day for in-patients. They include Princess Margaret Hospital, 2–10 Lai King Hill Rd, Lai Chi Kok, Kowloon ☎ 2990 1111; Queen Elizabeth Hospital, 30 Gascoigne Rd, Kowloon ☎ 3506 8888; and Queen Mary Hospital, Pok Fu Lam Rd, Hong Kong Island ☎ 2255 3838. Private hospitals are more expensive, but the standard of care is higher: Hong Kong Baptist Hospital, 222 Waterloo Rd, Kowloon Tong ☎ 2339 8888; Canossa Hospital, 1 Old Peak Rd, Hong Kong Island ☎ 2522 2181; Matilda Hospital, Suite 502, 39 Queen's Rd, Central ☎ 2537 8500.

Dentists are best contacted via the Hong Kong Dental Association (☻ hkda.org), but note treatment is expensive.

In Macau, 24hr medical emergencies are dealt with at the S. Januário

Hospital (government), Estrada do Visconde de S. Januário ☎ 2831 3731, or the Kiang Wu Hospital (private), Estrada Coelho do Amaral ☎ 2837 1333.

For non-urgent cases, head to the Tap Seac Health Centre, between Rua do Campo and Avenida Conselheiro Ferreira de Almeida ☎ 2852 2232. The region's only 24hr pharmacy is at the Caritas Medical Centre, 111 Wing Hong St, Sham Shui Po, Hong Kong (☎ 3408 5678). Watson's and Manning's (daily 9am–7pm or later) are ubiquitous Western-style pharmacies stocking toiletries and basic first-aid items. Products available over the counter here include contraceptive pills.

Internet

Free, fast wi-fi is available at the airports, most accommodation, many cafés (for paying customers) and shopping centres in both Hong Kong and Macau. Hong Kong's Central Library, south of Victoria Park, Causeway Bay (Mon, Tues & Thurs– Sun 10am–9pm, Wed 1–9pm) also offers free wi-fi, plus plenty of desk space for a laptop or tablet. In Macau, there's also a strong signal at many World Heritage-listed sites (most of the old town).

Laundry

Most accommodation offers (expensive) laundry services. Otherwise, there are laundries in almost every Hong Kong back street, charging by the weight of your washing – around HK$35 for a full bag – and taking a couple of hours.

Left luggage

Accommodation can often store luggage, but might have poor security and charge heavily too. Hong Kong has storage lockers at the airport, Airport Express stations, the China–Hong Kong Ferry Terminal (Kowloon), Hung Hom train station (Kowloon) and the Shun Tak Centre (Sheung Wan); in Macau, head to the Jetfoil Terminal. Expect to pay around HK$/MOP$90 per day.

Lost property

Contact the police or, in Hong Kong, offices at Admiralty Station, Tai Wai Station and Siu Hong Station (daily 8am–8pm; ☎ 2861 0020) for items left on trains; or call ☎ 1872920 for items left in taxis.

Massage

Golden Rock Acupressure and Massage Centre of the Blind (8/F, Golden Swan Building, 438 Hennessy Rd, Causeway Bay) and Charlie's Acupressure and Massage Centre of the Blind (Room 1103, Chung Sheung Building, 9–10 Queen Victoria St, Central ⓦ acupressuremassage.hk) charge $250 for the first hour, then $100 per thirty minutes to have your body pulled apart by a blind masseur.

A recommended foot masseur is Ten Feet Tall, 20–21/F, L Place, 139 Queen's Rd, Central, who charges $350 for a 50min reflexology session.

Money

Hong Kong dollars (HK$) come in HK$20, 50, 100, 500 and 1000 notes, and 10c, 20c, 50c, HK$1, 2, 5 and 10 coins. Many businesses won't accept HK$1000 bills. Macau uses the pataca (MOP$), made up of 100 avos. Notes come in denominations of MOP$10, 20, 50, 100, 500 and 1000, and coins come as 10, 20 and 50 avos, and MOP$1, 2, 5 and 10.

The pataca is worth three percent less than the Hong Kong dollar, and you can use Hong Kong dollars throughout Macau on a one-for-one basis. You can't use patacas in Hong Kong, however.

Both Hong Kong and Macau have an abundance of banks (Mon–Fri

9am–5pm, Sat 9am–noon) with 24hr ATMs accepting all major foreign credit and debit cards scattered through their downtown areas. Foreign banknotes can be cashed at banks (beware of high transaction fees), or private moneychangers, where you want to watch out for poor exchange rates. Credit cards are useful for high-end purchases but might attract a service charge, and many ordinary businesses (including cheaper restaurants and accommodation) accept cash only.

Opening hours and public holidays

Hong Kong's office hours are Monday to Friday 9am to 5pm, and Saturday 9am to 1pm; shops open daily 10am to 7pm or later in tourist areas; and post offices open Monday to Friday 9.30am to 5pm, Saturday 9.30am to 1pm. Museums often close one day a week. Temples have no set hours, opening daily from early morning to early evening; produce markets tend to kick off at dawn (when they're busiest) and peter out during the afternoon, though speciality markets (such as Temple Street Night Market) have varying opening times.

In Macau, government and official offices open Monday to Friday 8.30/9am to 1pm and 3 to 5/5.30pm, Saturday 8.30/9am to 1pm. Shops and businesses are usually open throughout the day and have slightly longer hours.

On **public holidays** and on some religious festivals most shops and all government offices in both Hong Kong and Macau are closed. For a list of public holidays visit ⓦ gov.hk/en/about/abouthk/holiday. See page 141 for details of festivals.

Phones

Local calls from private phones are free in Hong Kong and Macau. For international calls, it's cheapest to buy a discount phone card, where you dial an access number, enter a PIN supplied with the card, then dial the overseas number; costs to the UK, US or Australia are just a dollar or two per minute. Different cards give discounts for specific regions only, so you might have to shop around – Worldwide House in Central and Chungking Mansions in Tsim Sha Tsui (both in Hong Kong) have dozens of places selling them.

The same places also sell inexpensive prepaid local SIM cards for GSM-compatible phones, along with top-up vouchers. To call Macau from Hong Kong use the code +853; use +852 for the reverse.

Post

Hong Kong's post offices are open Monday to Friday between 9.30am and 5pm, and Saturday from 9.30am to 1pm. The General Post Office (GPO) is at 2 Connaught Place, Central, Hong Kong Island – poste restante will go here (collection Mon–Sat 8am–6pm); make sure you take your passport along. Airmail letters take around a week to reach Europe or North America.

Macau's GPO (Mon–Fri 9am–6pm, Sat 9am–1pm), where the poste restante mail is sent, is on Largo do Senado; there's also a post office at the Jetfoil Terminal (Mon–Sat 10am–7pm). Delivery times for letters to Europe and North America is the same as from Hong Kong.

Time

Hong Kong and Macau are eight hours ahead of GMT, thirteen hours ahead of New York, sixteen hours ahead of Los Angeles and two hours behind Sydney.

Tipping

In simple restaurants where there's no service charge, it's usual to leave a dollar or two (staff often give change from bills entirely in coins, hoping you'll leave it all). In taxis, make the fare up to the nearest dollar. Porters at upmarket hotels and at the airport require a tip – HK\$/MOP\$10 is usually ample.

Tourist information

The **Hong Kong Tourist Board** (daily 9am–6pm; ☎ 2508 1234, ⓦ discoverhongkong.com) is well informed about restaurants, accommodation, sights, tours and activities, as well as transport schedules; in addition, they organize free courses on tai chi, Cantonese opera, tea appreciation, pearl grading and more, for which you need to sign up a day in advance. Their downtown offices (daily 8am–8pm) are in the Star Ferry Terminal in Tsim Sha Tsui; and in an old railway carriage outside the Peak Mall, on The Peak.

The **Macau Government Tourist Office** (ⓦ macautourism.gov.mo) offers a limited range of brochures and advice. The main offices are at the Jetfoil Terminal (daily 9am–10pm), and in the centre of Macau at Largo do Senado 9 (daily 9am–6pm). At their Hong Kong office (Macau Ferry Terminal, Shun Tak Tower, Connaught Rd, Central; daily 9am–8pm; ☎ 2857 2287) you can usually get discounted rates for mid-range hotels prior to departure.

Travellers with disabilities

Hong Kong is reasonably accessible for travellers with disabilities. The Hong Kong Tourist Board's website includes an Accessible Hong Kong page (ⓦ discoverhongkong.com) with links to Hong Kong websites for disabled travellers.

Macau is far less easy to negotiate for physically disabled travellers. The streets are older, narrower, rougher and steeper, and it lacks the overhead ramps and wide, modern elevators that make Hong Kong relatively approachable. Contact the Macau Tourist Office (ⓦ macautourism.gov.mo) before you travel for details of accommodation and transport facilities.

Travelling with children

The Chinese are very child-friendly people as a rule, and make a lot of fuss over both their own offspring and other peoples. In addition, both Hong Kong and Macau have abundant attractions – Ocean Park, Disneyland, Hong Kong Wetland Park, Kadoorie Farm, plus a host of museums, temples, festivals, food, shopping and tours – to keep the little ones entertained, many with reduced entry prices for children or families. There are also plenty of supermarkets and chemists with English-speaking staff, where it's possible to find familiar brands of formula, nappies and child medicines.

Some restaurants – most usually Western ones – have child menus, while others might allow you to order half portions; having children in tow, especially young ones, might also secure you half-decent table service. Many of the better hotels offer child-minding services, and public washrooms in urban shopping malls often have changing facilities. Don't breast-feed in public. Things to guard against are the exhausting tropical heat and humidity, poor hygiene, the bustling crowds and constant noise – though frankly these seem to stress out parents more than their children.

Festivals and events

Chinese traditional festival dates are fixed by the lunar calendar, which follows the phases of the moon and is therefore out of step with the Western calendar. We've indicated the likely months in which the following festivals will occur; check with the Hong Kong or Macau tourist offices for specific dates.

Chinese New Year (Spring Festival)

January/February

Celebrated for the first two weeks of the first month of the lunar calendar. Red and gold decorations, flower markets, lion and dragon dances, and colossal firework displays in both Hong Kong and Macau set the tone. The best public spot to see Hong Kong's harbourside fireworks is at the bottom end of Nathan Road in Tsim Sha Tsui; in Macau it's by the lake on Avenida da Praia Grande – check local papers or tourist office websites for dates. Temples are packed out, too, and families get together to celebrate and eat special "lucky" New Year foods, such as noodles (for long life), fish (because the Chinese word sounds the same as that for "surplus") and crescent dumplings (symbolizing wealth).

Yuen Siu (Spring Lantern Festival)

January/February

Marks the last day of the Chinese New Year (the fifteenth day of the first moon). Brightly coloured paper lanterns symbolizing the moon are hung in parks, shops, temples and houses. There's a second lantern festival in September; see "Mid-Autumn Festival" on page 143. Good places to see elaborate arrangements are Victoria and Kowloon parks in Hong Kong, and on the steps of São Paulo in Macau.

Ching Ming

April

At the beginning of the third moon, this is also known as "Grave-sweeping day". Families head to old cemeteries up in the hills to burn incense and paper cars, houses, "hell" money and even food at ancestral graves, while prayers are said for the departed souls and blessings sought for the latest generations of the family.

Tin Hau/A-Ma Festival

April/May

Festival to honour the protective goddess of the sea (known as Tin Hau in Hong Kong and as A-Ma in Macau), held on the 23rd day of the third lunar month. Fishing boats are colourfully decorated with flags, streamers and pennants, as fishermen and others who follow the goddess gather at Tin Hau temples (especially at Clearwater Bay) to ask for luck and to offer food, fruit and pink dumplings.

Tam Kung Festival

April/May

Honours another patron saint of fishermen on the eighth day of the fourth lunar month, at the temple in Shau Kei Wan on Hong Kong Island.

Tai Chiu (Cheung Chau Bun) Festival

April/May

A week-long extravaganza on Cheung Chau Island, with dances, operas, martial arts shows, parades and towers of steamed buns, held to pacify the ghosts of those killed in former times by Cheung Chau's pirates. In deference to the religious nature of the event, no meat is served on the island during this time. The focus is Cheung Chau's Pak Tai Temple, and highlights are the afternoon "floating children" parade on the fifth day, and the scaling of the immense bun tower the following midnight by teams who compete to grab the most buns.

Buddha's Birthday

May

A low-key celebration when Buddha's statue is taken out of the various

香港文化中心 Hong Kong Cultural Centre
香港迪士尼樂園 Hong Kong Disneyland
香港文化博物館 Hong Kong Heritage Museum
香港歷史博物館 Hong Kong History Museum
香港公園 Hong Kong Park
香港鐵路博物館 Hong Kong Railway Museum
香港科學館 Hong Kong Science Museum
香港濕地公園 Hong Kong Wetland Park
洪聖廟 Hung Shing Temple
環球貿易廣場 ICC
國際金融中心二期 IFC2
玉器市場 Jade Market
嘉道理農場 Kadoorie Farm
吉慶圍圍村 Kat Hing Wai Walled Village
九龍公園 Kowloon Park
九龍寨城公園 Kowloon Walled City Park
女人街 Ladies' Market
林村許願樹 Lam Tsuen Wishing Trees
立法會大樓 LEGCO building
李鄭屋漢墓 Lei Chung Uk Han Tomb Museum
力寶中心 Lippo Centre
獅子山（郊野公園）Lion Rock (Country Park)
香港文華東方酒店 Mandarin Oriental Hotel
文武廟 Man Mo Temple
半山自動扶梯 Mid-Levels Escalator
香港藝術館 Museum of Art
香港海防博物館 Museum of Coastal Defence
茶具文物館 Museum of Teaware
南蓮園池 Nan Lian Gardens
午砲 Noon Day Gun
香港海洋公園 Ocean Park
北帝廟 Pak Tai Temple
八仙嶺郊野公園 Pat Sin Leng Country Park
山頂 The Peak
半島酒店 The Peninsula Hotel
寶蓮寺 Po Lin Monastery
三太子宮 Sam Tai Tze Temple
石壁水塘 Shek Pik Reservoir
上窰民俗文物館 Sheung Yiu Folk Museum

信德中心 Shun Tak Centre
嗇色園 Sik Sik Yuen Temple
香港太空館 Space Museum
皇后像廣場 Statue Square
大埔滘自然護理區 Tai Po Kau Nature Reserve
廟街夜市 Temple Street Night Market
萬佛寺 Ten Thousand Buddhas Monastery
天壇大佛 Tian Tan Big Buddha
時代廣場 Times Square
天后廟 Tin Hau Temple
曾大屋圍村 Tsang Tai Uk Walled Village
維多利亞公園 Victoria Park
西港城 Western Market
香港動植物公園 Zoological and Botanical Gardens

Streets

界限街 Boundary Street
寶雲道 Bowen Road
廣東道 Canton Road
德輔道 Des Voeux Road
告士打道 Gloucester Road
加連威老街 Granville Road
軒尼詩道 Hennessy Road
荷李活道 Hollywood Road
蘭桂坊 Lan Kwai Fong
利源東/西街 Li Yuen Street (east/west)
駱克道 Lockhart Road
南固臺 Nam Koo Terrace
彌敦道 Nathan Road
砵典乍街 Pottinger Street
皇后大道 Queen's Road
皇后東大道 Queen's Road East
新填地街 Reclamation Street
上海街 Shanghai Street
太原街 Tai Yuen Street

Transport

巴士站 Bus stop
赤鱲角機場 Hong Kong International Airport
中港碼頭 China Ferry Terminal
輕便鐵路車站 LR station
纜車總站 Lower Peak Tram Terminal
港澳碼頭 Macau Ferry Terminal
地下鐵車站 MTR station
昂坪360 Ngong Ping 360
港外線碼頭 Outlying Islands Ferry Pier
天星碼頭 Star Ferry Pier

Macau Sightseeing

Places

媽閣 Barra
路環 Coloane
澳門 Macau
外港 Porto Exterior
內港 Porto Interior
冰仔 Taipa

Sights

媽閣廟 A-Ma Temple
基督教墳場 Cemitério Protestante
竹灣 Cheoc Van
路環市區 Coloane Village
澳門漁人碼頭 Fishermans' Wharf
東望洋山堡壘 Fortaleza da Guia
大炮台 Fortaleza do Monte
松山 Guia Hill
黑沙海灘 Hác Sá Beach
康公廟 Hong Kung Temple
葡京酒店 Lisboa Hotel
盧廉若公園 Jardim Lou Lim Ieoc
白鴿巢賈梅士花園 Jardim Luís de Camões
觀音堂 Kun Iam Temple
議事亭前地 Largo do Senado
議事亭 Leal Senado
蓮峰廟 Lin Fong Temple
連溪廟 Lin Kai Temple
澳門文化中心 Macau Cultural Centre
澳門博物館 Museu de Macau
林則徐博物館 Museu Lin Zexu
海事博物館 Museu Maritimo
北帝廟 Pak Tai Temple
石排灣郊野公園 Parque de Seac Pai Van
主教山教堂 Penha Chapel
關閘 Portas de Cerco
聖地牙哥 Pousada de São Tiago
港局大樓 Quartel dos Mouros
紅街市 Red Market
路環聖方濟各教堂 St Francis Xavier Chapel
仁慈堂大樓 Santa Casa de Misericórdia
聖澳斯定教堂 Santo Agostinho
聖母玫瑰堂 São Domingos
大三巴牌坊 São Paulo
大堂 Sé
冰仔舊城區 Taipa Village
伯多祿五世劇院 Teatro dom Pedro V

三盞燈 Three Lamps District
天后古廟 Tin Hau Temple
威尼斯人度假村 The Venetian

Streets

友誼大馬路 Avenida da Amizade
民國大馬路 Avenida da Republica
新馬路 Avenida de Almeida Ribeiro
南灣大馬路 Praia Grande
龍嵩正街 Rua Central
福隆新街 Rua da Felicidade
草堆街 Rua das Estalagens
十月初五街 Rua de Cinco de Outubro
河邊新街 Rua do Almirante Sérgio
板樟堂街 Rua Sul do Mercado de São Domingos

Transport

蛇口碼頭 China Ferry Terminal
港澳碼頭 Jetfoil Terminal
澳門機場 Macau Airport

Useful words

Some Cantonese signs

入口 Entrance
出口 Exit
廁所 Toilets
男廁 Gentlemen
女廁 Ladies
營業中 Open
休業 Closed
到達 Arrivals
出發 Departures
休假 Closed for holidays
出故障 Out of order
礦泉水 Drinking/mineral water
請勿吸煙 No Smoking
危險 Danger
關稅 Customs
公共汽車 Bus
渡船 Ferry
火車 Train
飛幾場 Airport
警察 Police
飯店 Restaurant
賓館 Hotel
野營位置 Campsite
海灘 Beach
禁止游泳 No Swimming

Some Portuguese words

Alfândega Customs
Avenida Avenue
Baía Bay
Beco Alley
Bilheteira Ticket office
Calçada Cobbled street
Correios Post office
Edifício Building
Estrada Road
Farmácia Pharmacy
Farol Lighthouse
Fortaleza Fortress
Hospedaria Guesthouse
Jardim Garden
Largo Square
Lavabos Toilets
Mercado Market
Museu Museum
Pensão Guesthouse
Ponte Bridge
Pousada Inn/Hotel
Praça Square
Praia Beach
Rua Street
Sé Cathedral
Travessa Lane
Vila Guesthouse

Hong Kong menu reader

General

我食齋 I'm vegetarian
菜單/英文菜單 Menu/English menu
筷子 Chopsticks
刀叉/匙羹 Knife/fork/spoon
埋單 Bill/cheque

Drinks

啤酒 Beer
咖啡 Coffee
(礦泉) 水 (Mineral) Water
葡萄酒 Wine
白酒 Spirits
豆漿 Soya milk
茶 Tea
紅茶 Black tea
綠茶 Green tea
鐵觀音茶 "Iron Buddha" tea
香片茶 Jasmine tea
普洱茶 Bo lei tea
苦茶 Medicinal tea
五花茶 Five-flower tea
甘四味茶 Twenty-four flavour tea

Staple foods

竹筍 Bamboo shoots
芽菜 Bean sprouts
豆角 Beans
牛肉 Beef
牛肉丸 Beef ball
豆豉醬 Black bean sauce
雞 Chicken
辣椒 Chilli
菜心 Chinese greens
蟹 Crab
青瓜 Cucumber
鴨 Duck
鰻 Eel
魚 Fish
蒜頭 Garlic
薑 Ginger
鵝 Goose
青椒 Green pepper
羊肉 Lamb
味精 MSG
磨菇 Mushrooms
麵條 Noodles
蠔油 Oyster sauce
白鴿 Pigeon
豬肉 Pork
大蝦 Prawns
蝦丸 Prawn balls
河粉 Rice noodles
白飯 Rice, boiled
鹽 Salt
芝麻油 Sesame oil
湯 Soup
豉油 Soy sauce
魚 Squid
糖 Sugar
豆腐 Tofu/Beancurd
醋 Vinegar
白蘿卜 White radish

Cooking methods

焙 Casseroled
沙鍋 Claypot/sandpot
煮 Boiled
炒 Fried

Dim sum menu reader

Savouries

Steamed prawn dumplings 蝦餃
Steamed beef ball 山竹牛肉
Steamed spare ribs 排骨
Steamed pork and prawn dumpling 燒賣
Steamed bun stuffed with barbecued pork 叉燒飽
Steamed chicken bun 雞飽
Steamed rice-flour roll stuffed with beef 牛肉腸粉
Steamed rice packet stuffed with chicken,
wrapped in a lotus leaf 糯米雞
Deep-fried wonton with sweet and sour sauce 炸雲吞
Congee (rice porridge, flavoured with shredded meat 粥 and vegetables)
Spring roll 春卷
Radish cake 蘿蔔糕
Chicken feet 鳳爪
Stuffed green peppers 煎釀青椒
Taro/yam croquette 芋角
Prawn rice roll 蝦腸粉
Shark's fin dumplings* 魚翅餃
Steamed fishballs 鯪魚球
Crispy-fried squid tentacles 炸魷魚鬚
Fried rice-flour ball stuffed with meat 咸水角
Deep-fried beancurd roll with pork/shrimp 鮮竹卷
Crystal-skinned dumpling 潮洲粉果
"Thousand-year" preserved eggs 皮蛋
*named after the shape – they don't contain shark's fin

Sweets

Cold beancurd with syrup 豆腐花
Coconut jelly 椰汁糕
Steamed sponge cake 馬拉糕
Mango pudding 芒果布甸
Sweet lotus-seed paste bun 蓮蓉飽
Egg-custard tart 蛋撻

白煮 Poached
烤 Roast
蒸 Steamed
清炒 Stir-fried

Main Dishes

叉燒 （飯） Barbecued pork (on rice)
豆腐湯 Beancurd soup
牛肉丸湯 Beef ball soup
燉鴨素菜 Braised duck with vegetables
客家豆腐 Casseroled beancurd stuffed with pork mince
筍尖嫩玉米炒雞片 Chicken with bamboo shoots and baby corn

腰果雞丁 Chicken with cashew nuts
蠔油芥蘭 Chinese broccoli in oyster sauce
沙鍋腊腸飯 Claypot rice with sweet sausage
豉汁焗蟹 Crab with black beans
燒肉(飯) Crisp-skinned pork (on rice)
蛋炒飯 Egg fried rice
魚丸湯 Fish ball soup
焙魚 Fish casserole
清蒸魚 Fish steamed with ginger and spring onion
豆腐素菜 Fried beancurd with vegetables
炒豆芽 Fried bean sprouts

檸檬雞 Lemon chicken
羅漢齋 Monks' dish (stir-fry of vegetables and fungi)
湯麵 Noodle soup
蒜頭炒蝦 Prawn with garlic sauce
燒鴨(飯) Roast duck (on rice)
燒鵝 Roast goose
客家鹽幾 Salt-baked chicken
豆豉青椒炒魚 Squid with green pepper and black beans
豆豉蒸鰻 Steamed eel with black beans
清炒竹筍 Stir-fried bamboo shoots
筍尖炒雞片 Stir-fried chicken and bamboo shoots
糖醋排骨 Sweet and sour spare ribs
雲吞湯 Wonton soup

Macau menu reader

General

Almoço Lunch
Comidas Meals/dishes
Jantar Dinner
Prato do dia/Menu Dish/menu of the **do dia** day

Basics and snacks

Arroz Rice
Batatas fritas French fries
Legumes Vegetables
Manteiga Butter
Omeleta Omelette
Ovos Eggs
Pimenta Pepper
Prego Steak roll
Sal Salt
Salada mista Mixed salad
Sandes Sandwiches

Meat

Almôndegas Meatballs
Bife Steak
Chouriço Spicy sausage
Coelho Rabbit
Cordoniz Quail
Costeleta Chop, cutlet
Dobrada Tripe stew
Fígado Liver
Galinha Chicken
Pombo Pigeon

Porco Pork
Salsicha Sausage

Fish and seafood

Amêijoas Clams
Bacalhau Dried, salted cod
Camarões Shrimp
Carangueijo Crab
Gambas Prawns
Linguado Sole
Lulas Squid
Mexilhões Mussels
Pescada Hake
Sardinhas Sardines

Soups

Caldo verde Green cabbage and potato soup, often served with spicy sausage
Sopa álentejana Garlic and bread soup with a poached egg
Sopa de mariscos Shellfish soup
Sopa de peixe Fish soup

Cooking terms

Assado Roasted
Cozido Boiled, stewed
Frito Fried
Grelhado Grilled
No forno Baked

Specialities

Camarões Huge grilled prawns with chillies and peppers
Cataplana Seafood with bacon, sausage and peppers
Cozido á Boiled casserole **Portuguesa** of mixed meats, rice and vegetables
Galinha á Africana Chicken baked with **(African chicken)** peppers and chillies
Galinha á Chicken baked **Portuguesa** with eggs, potatoes, onion and saffron in a curry sauce
Feijoada Rich stew of beans, pork, sausage and vegetables
Pasteis de Cod fishcakes, **bacalhau** deep-fried
Porco á álentejana Pork and clams in a stew
Pudim flán Creme caramel
Arroz doce Portuguese rice pudding

Drinks

Água mineral Mineral water
Café Coffee
Chá Tea
Cerveja Beer
Sumo de laranja Orange juice

Vinho tinto Red wine
Vinho branco White wine
Vinho do Porto Port (both red and white)
Vinho verde young wine, slightly sparkling and refreshing; usually white

Glossary

A–Ma see "Tin Hau".
ancestral hall temple hall where ancestral records and shrines are kept.
BOC Bank of China.
dim sum Cantonese-style breakfast made up of a selection of small soups, dumplings and special dishes, served with tea. Also known as *yum cha*.
feng shui the belief that the arrangement of local landscape affects an area or building's "luck".
gweilo European, foreigner.
Hakka Chinese ethnic group who live in distinctive clan villages.
Handover the formal handing back of Hong Kong by Britain to China in 1997.
HKTB Hong Kong Tourist Board.
HSBC Hongkong and Shanghai Bank.
ICC International Commerce Centre – Hong Kong's tallest building.
IFC2 International Finance Centre, Tower 2.
Kwun Yam the Chinese Boddhisattva of Mercy, especially prayed to by women wanting children and safe childbirth.

LEGCO Hong Kong's Legislative Council.
Mainland China, excepting Hong Kong and Macau.
MTR Mass Transit Railway – Hong Kong's urban rail network.
New Territories the area of Hong Kong between Kowloon and the Chinese border.
New Towns self-contained satellite towns spread across the New Territories, designed to decentralize Hong Kong's urban population.
pastelaria Macanese sweet/savouries shop specializing in almond biscuits, peanut brittle and roast meats.
SAR Special Administrative Region of China, hence "Hong Kong SAR" and "Macau SAR". Though technically controlled by the Chinese government, SARs enjoy considerably more local autonomy and freedoms than is permitted on the mainland.
Tin Hau sea goddess and protector of fishermen; known as A-Ma in Macau.
Triad Organized crime gang, similar to the Mafia.
yum cha see "*dim sum*".

Publishing Information
Fourth edition 2019

Distribution
UK, Ireland and Europe
Apa Publications (UK) Ltd; sales@roughguides.com
United States and Canada
Ingram Publisher Services; ips@ingramcontent.com
Australia and New Zealand
Woodslane; info@woodslane.com.au
Southeast Asia
Apa Publications (SN) Pte; sales@roughguides.com
Worldwide
Apa Publications (UK) Ltd; sales@roughguides.com
Special Sales, Content Licensing and CoPublishing
Rough Guides can be purchased in bulk quantities at discounted prices. We can create special editions, personalised jackets and corporate imprints tailored to your needs. sales@roughguides.com.
roughguides.com
Printed in Hong Kong by RR Donnelley Asia Printing Solutions Limited

A catalogue record for this book is available from the British Library
The publishers and authors have done their best to ensure the accuracy and currency of all the information in **Pocket Rough Guide Hong Kong and Macau**, however, they can accept no responsibility for any loss, injury, or inconvenience sustained by any traveller as a result of information or advice contained in the guide.

Rough Guide Credits
Editor: Aimee White
Cartography: Ed Wright
Managing editor: Rachel Lawrence
Picture editor: Aude Vauconsant
Cover photo research: Phoebe Lowndes

Original design: Richard Czapnik
Senior DTP coordinator: Dan May
Head of DTP and Pre-Press: Rebeka Davies

Author: David Leffman first visited Hong Kong in 1985 and seems to have spent most of his life since contributing to books about the Chinese world. He has a degree in photography and studied Mandarin Chinese at SOAS, London and Sichuan University, China. He has also co-authored and edited guidebooks to Australia, China, Indonesia, Hong Kong, Iceland and Malaysia for Rough Guides, Dorling Kindersley and others.

SMALL PRINT

Photo Credits

(Key: T-top; C-centre; B-bottom; L-left; R-right)

Index

A

Aberdeen 58
addresses 137
Afternoon tea 65
A-Ma Temple 117
arrival 134
Avenida da Amizade 119

B

bars and clubs
  All Night Long 75
  Bit Point 46
  Café Gray Deluxe 56
  Carnegie's 56
  Club 71 46
  Club Qing 46
  Dada Bar 75
  Delaney's 75
  Devil's Advocate 56
  Dickens Sports Bar 57
  Dragon-i 46
  Dusk Till Dawn 57
  Fringe Club 46
  Havana Bar 47
  Insomnia 47
  Joe Banana's 57
  Keg sports bar 47
  Magnum Club 47
  Ned Kelly's Last Stand 75
  Origin 47
  Peel Fresco Music Lounge 47
  TED's Lookout 57
  Tequila Jack's 75
  Vibes 75
  Volar 47
  Wanch 57
bars and clubs (by area)
  Hong Kong Island: Wan Chai,
    Causeway Bay and Happy
    Valley 56
  Hong Kong Island, Central to
    Kennedy Town 46
  Kowloon: Tsim Sha Tsui 75
Bowen Road 49
buses 136
by air 134
by bus 135
by ferry 134
by train 135

C

Canton Road 64
Casinos 116
Cemitério Protestante 111
Central Plaza 48
Che Kung Temple 90

Cheung Chau 106
Chi Lin Nunnery 82
China's martial arts 70
chronology 143
cinema 137
Clearwater Bay 94
Coloane 121
Cotai 120
crime 137

D

Des Voeux Road 32
directory A-Z 137

E

electricity 138
Elevated walkways 31
embassies and consulates 138
emergency numbers 138
Exchange Square 27

F

Feng shui 34
ferries 136
festivals and events 141
  Birthday of Confucius 143
  Birthday of Lo Pan 143
  Buddha's Birthday 142
  Cheung Yeung Festival 143
  Chinese New Year (Spring
    Festival) 142
  Ching Ming 142
  Maidens' Festival 143
  Mid-Autumn Festival 143
  Tai Chiu (Cheung Chau Bun)
    Festival 142
  Tam Kung Festival 142
  Tin Hau/A-Ma Festival 142
  Tuen Ng (Dragon Boat) Festival
    143
  Yue Lan Festival 143
  Yuen Siu (Spring Lantern
    Festival) 142
Flower Market 80
Fortaleza de São Tiago da
  Barra 118
Fortaleza do Monte 110

G

getting around 135
Goldfish Market 77
Government House 34
Guia Hill 113

H

Happy Valley Racecourse 51
Harbourfront Promenade 27
health 138
Hollywood Road 36
Hong Kong, an Opium War
  trophy 30
Hong Kong Disneyland 98
Hong Kong History Museum 69
Hong Kong Island: Central to
  Kennedy Town 26
Hong Kong Island: the south
  side 58
Hong Kong Island: Wan Chai,
  Causeway Bay and Happy
  Valley 48
Hong Kong Park 34
Hong Kong Science Museum
  70
Hong Kong Wetland Park 88
Hong Kung Temple 110

I

IFC2 27
internet 139

J

Jardim Lou Lim Ieoc 112
Jardim Luís de Camões 111

K

Kadoorie Farm 94
Kam Tin 87
Kennedy Town 40
Kowloon: Jordan to Diamond
  Hill 76
Kowloon: Tsim Sha Tsui 64
Kowloon Park 70
Kowloon Walled City Park 81
Kun Iam Temple 114

L

Ladies' Market 77
Lamma 104
Lamma and Cheung Chau 104
Lam Tsuen Wishing Trees 93
Land reclamation 117
language 145
Lan Kwai Fong 33
Lantau 98
Lantau Peak 99
Largo do Senado 108
left luggage 139

NOTES